The Lord be with you

A Parish Priest speaks with his people

Cormac Rigby

FAMILY PUBLICATIONS

OXFORD

The publisher and the author wish to express their gratitude to those friends and parishioners who kindly allowed the use of their photographs in this book.

First printed January 2004

Reprinted March 2004

ISBN 1-871217-42-3 (paperback)

ISBN 1-871217-43-1 (hardback)

published by

FAMILY PUBLICATIONS

6a King Street, Oxford, OX2 6DF

www.familypublications.co.uk

printed in England by

Cromwell Press, Trowbridge, Wilts.

Contents

Yours
is to nourish them
with word and sacrament
so that in accordance
with THEIR vocation
THEY may be
Christ's presence in the world.

Cardinal Hume
Chrism Mass, 1989

Foreword

Many will find this collection of sermons to be of great help to them, both in their understanding of the faith and in their search for God.

Fr Cormac brings his undoubted gifts to these homilies. He has a warm heart and he understands us in all our frailty. He has a clear head. He has studied and entered into the teachings of the Church. He expounds them for us with great clarity. This is particularly true of his presentation of the teachings of the Church about the Mass.

He has a rich experience. He is a man who has travelled, who has studied history, has a great love of music and ballet, is familiar with great poetry and literature. All of these sources enrich and illustrate his homilies.

He also had many years as a BBC presenter. This encouraged him in the drafting and shaping of scripts. He is a wordsmith and his presentations can enthral us.

In addition, those who know him personally will be able to imagine these homilies spoken with his rich and attractive voice. Listening to him is so easy on the ear. It means that we can more easily give our attention to what he is saying.

Many who read this book will, I am sure, be moved to offer a prayer for Fr Cormac as he lives with the experience of illness. It is true to say that a priest never retires. In an image that he himself uses in these texts, he is still a paschal candle burning before the Lord, to mark out, point out the presence of our loving Lord.

Vincent Nichols

+ *Vincent Nichols,*
Archbishop of Birmingham

*Fr Cormac waits for the arrival of the bride at his last
Nuptial Mass at St William of York, 27 September 2003.
Ann-Marie Dwyer was marrying Maurizio Bibbo.*

About the author

Several orbits interact in the life of Cormac Rigby, and all meet in these wonderfully crafted sermons whose simplicity conceals the range of experience on which they draw. As a lifelong friend of Cormac, I have been privileged to follow his various journeys. He was born in Watford in 1939. From Merchant Taylors' School where we were contemporaries, he went like me to St John's College, Oxford, where he read History. It was here, largely thanks to Cormac, that I became a Catholic. After a failed attempt to study for the priesthood in Rome, he returned to do research at St John's. His doctoral thesis was on Edward Thring, the celebrated Victorian teacher who hosted the first Headmasters' Conference at Uppingham.

In 1965, while I started my academic career, Cormac joined BBC radio as an announcer, and for fourteen years, from 1971 to 1985, was the Presentation Editor of Radio 3, leading its team of announcers, and continuously concerned with the standards of broadcast English. Since the 'sixties he has derived most pleasure from the world of ballet. His series *Royal Repertoire* ran throughout the 'seventies on Radio 3. He used the pen name John Cowan to write about ballet in *Dance and Dancers* and the *Oxford Mail*. After leaving the BBC he wrote regularly under his own name for the quarterly *Dance Now*, and presented ballet programmes for Radio 2 and BBC World Service.

His final *Last Night of the Proms* was in 1985, and on 21 May 1988, Cardinal Basil Hume ordained him in Westminster Cathedral. He spent eleven years as Assistant Priest at Most Sacred Heart Church, Ruislip, during which time he and his sister Deirdre also provided 24-hour care and support for their ailing mother until her death. There were occasional returns to the microphone. He has narrated for performances by David Titterington and Dame Gillian Weir of works by Petr Eben and Olivier Messiaen. He and Hannah Gordon were the two readers on the BBC Philharmonic recording of Britten's *The World of the Spirit,* now on a Chandos CD. He introduced the bicentennial performance of Mozart's *Requiem* at St Stephen's Cathedral in Vienna, and the memorial Mass for Lennox Berkeley; and in

June 1999 he provided the commentary on Radio 3's relay of the Requiem Mass for Cardinal Hume at Westminster Cathedral.

That same summer he took over as Parish Priest of St William of York, Stanmore, where he was deeply happy until forced by ill health to retire in September 2003. He has now returned to live in North Oxford.

Of the various orbits influencing Cormac's life, I would highlight three: the precision and clarity that is the hallmark of the best of BBC presentation; the subtle sensibility from the world of performing arts; and, above all, the sense of the all-pervasiveness of the Gospel that can only come from a deep and constantly lived spirituality. All of these can be found in these sermons. Fr Cormac's gentle probing of the meaning of the Gospel is always based on the personal. It has been said that to be a relevant leader you must say something eternal. Fr Cormac's sermons do this *par excellence:* they unite the personal with the universal message. They deal with life's most important and abiding questions, but are direct and easy to read. St Augustine tells us that his conversion was prompted by hearing a child in his garden singing *'tolle lege, tolle lege'*, 'take and read, take and read'. Reader, you have taken up this book; read on, to the end.

> *David McLellan*
> *Professor of Political Theory*
> *University of Kent*

Preface

These sermon texts were written for the spoken word. They were not designed to be models of written English. In my final long-hand drafts, the scripts tend to look fragmented – more like clusters of words than conventional prose. Quite like radio scripts in fact. But those who heard them – and frequently assumed they were impromptu – often asked for 'the notes' so that they could revisit the ideas and insights on offer. They were often surprised to discover it was all written down. That is how they come to appear in book form now, minimally adapted. They are just the ordinary Sunday sermons of a Parish Priest trying to explore the Gospel and hoping that his own experiences and insights might strike a chord with his hearers.

Cormac Rigby
Oxford, December 2003

The Son of Man must be lifted up
so that everyone who believes
may have eternal life.

I am Cormac,
The son of Grace & Ted.

When I was born
in the nursing home in King Street in Watford
an identity tag was put on my wrist
— my Mother kept it for years.
It simply said 'Baby Rigby'.
That was on the 5th of May.
On the 21st
— which was my father's birthday —
I became Cormac.

I was baptised & christened
in the church of Our Lady Help of Christians
in Ricky,

by a French priest
who had queried
whether there had ever been
a real Christian saint
with the name Cormac.

The choice of name was very deliberate.
Before her marriage
my Mother was Grace McCormack
& once she had changed her name
to the English Rigby
she was determined
to regain possession of it
through her first-born son.
So Cormac was my Christian name.

*After the drafting and the editing, a manuscript fair copy
emerges in a layout which helps the preacher in the pulpit.*

Chapter 1

The Son of Man must be lifted up so that
everyone who believes may have eternal life.

I am Cormac, the son of Grace and Ted.

When I was born in the nursing home in King Street
in Watford, an identity tag was put on my wrist –
my mother kept it for years. It simply said 'Baby Rigby'.

That was on the 5th of May. On the 21st –
which was my father's birthday – I became Cormac.

I was baptised and christened in the church of
Our Lady Help of Christians in Rickmansworth,
by a French priest who had queried whether there had
ever been a real Christian saint with the name Cormac.

The choice of name was very deliberate.
Before her marriage my mother was Grace McCormack,
and once she had changed her name to the English 'Rigby'
she was determined to regain possession of it
through her first-born son.

So Cormac was my Christian name.
And just in case so unusual a name
might become an embarrassment to me at school,
I was called John as well – a sort of fall-back position.

In fact I have lived my life, both as Cormac and as John,
very happily. John was to become meaningful in my life later on:
it became my *nom de plume* when I ventured into journalism,
and was the name and identity
of the friend who most shaped my life.

Cormac is a great name to have. A *Christian* name certainly.

Saint Cormac was both a king and bishop in Ireland and
the ruins of his chapel survive to this day on the Rock of Cashel.
His feast day is the 14th September and I've always tried
to celebrate it with great affection and loyalty.

Eighteen years ago, when I left the BBC to study for
the priesthood, my final continuity shift and my last
Outside Broadcast – the Last Night of the Proms –
were on the 14th of September, the feast of St Cormac.

And now, after fifteen years as a priest, my final Sunday
as a parish priest is 14th of September, feast of St Cormac.

Is this just sentimental coincidence? I think not.
It is providential that the significance of my Christian name
has come to mean so much to me.

When we are baptised we enter by name
into the sacramental life, we begin our journey
into the world of the spirit, and we are named, identified.
Our Christian name is the proclamation that
each one of us is known to God in a unique way.

I am not just 'Baby Rigby' who became 'Father Rigby'.
I am Cormac; and it is by that treasured name
that I am uniquely known to God.

And so it is with all of you.
You are not mere statistics, you are not just population,
you are chosen by God, and your name is the symbol
of his choice.

I do beg you always, year by year, to celebrate your
Christian name because it proclaims your unique value
in the sight of God.

Every time I sign my Christian name, it is an act of faith
and an act of love. Each time I celebrate the feast of St Cormac
it is a response to the Grace which began
to flow into my life through baptism.

As it so happens, St Cormac's Day is also the birthday
of a much-loved friend, and so I can hardly avoid
a tremendous sense of being alive every 14th of September.

If that were all, it would be a happy day indeed.
But there is more.

September 14th is also the feast of the Holy Cross.
As a boy I went to Holy Rood School in Watford where
my mother Grace taught for many years. Rood is the
Anglo-Saxon word for cross, and in that beautiful church
there is a magnificent rood beam: high above the altar-rails
are the figure of Christ on the cross, and the grieving figures
of his mother and his dearest friend, John.

At first glance it seems a representation of human failure
and tragedy: a dead prophet, a defeated saint.
But what makes it not a tragedy but a triumph
is that on the third day he rose again.

Hatred had nailed him to the cross.
But he looked down from it and saw the total love for Him
in Mary and John – and he gave each of them to the other.
Then he looked out beyond them
and saw the gang of soldiers who had crucified him,
and beyond them the hostile mob,
and beyond them again the millions of sinners
whose individual sins had clustered together and nailed him
to the cross. And he said:

    'Father, forgive them; they know not what they do.'

These are the most important words ever uttered.
They are the Triumph of Love over Hate.
They are the Triumph of Forgiveness,
They are the Triumph of the Cross.

It was not a great general absolution,
not a worldwide gesture of reconciliation.
No – just as in our baptism we are uniquely named
and claimed by God, so too we uniquely and individually
fail and turn away from God.
Each of us makes choices which alienate us from love.
And then, uniquely and individually, we come into
the sight of Christ, and He can see each one of us
with the absolute clarity of God.

And He says: 'Cormac, I love you. Cormac, I forgive you.'
That is what our faith means: the love of God is for individuals,
the forgiveness of God is for individuals –
you and me. By name.

He knows us better than we know ourselves,
his love is undeterred by our failures,
he reaches down to us from the cross,
he holds our hand as he rises from the dead
and promises to take us with him.

The Son of Man must be lifted up on the cross,
so that everyone who believes in the survival of Love
may have eternal life.

We who are uniquely named are uniquely redeemed,
and as I celebrate St Cormac and the Feast of the Holy Rood
I see in them the truth that nothing, neither life nor death,
can separate us from the love of God.

Chapter 2

A man's words flow from what fills his heart.

I once heard a somewhat charismatic deacon saying
that when he preached, he never prepared for it:
'I just open my mouth and let the Holy Spirit
speak through me.'

And he felt he was justified in that policy because
when Our Lord warned his disciples that they were liable
to be hauled up before courts and judges, he told them
not to worry about what to say
because the Holy Spirit would inspire them.

And I'm sure that's right.
When you read the trials of Jesuit martyrs
like Edmund Campion and Robert Southwell
you find them exhausted after torture,
having to face panels of Protestant divines
and still well able to defend the faith.

But I'm not sure that that justifies us in leaving
everything to the Holy Spirit.
What did Our Lord really mean?
At daily Mass, I usually say a few words at the outset;
no script, and no notes, just a brief introduction,
so that when the readings happen
there'll be a particular point to listen out for.

But on Sundays – as you'll have noticed –
I always have my sermon in front of me, because
I believe that you are entitled to hear, not my first thoughts,
but my considered thoughts on whatever it is.

Thinking aloud is not preaching the Gospel.
At best thinking aloud is only work-in-progress,
and I don't think I should try to pin that on the Holy Spirit.

It's not my thinking aloud which is of interest to you,
but the results of my thinking.
When I have thought about it, and prayed about it,
and tried to get it into some sort of coherent shape,
then, and only then, should I put it in front of you.

Yes, I have seen priests in pulpits with no notes,
and sometimes it sounds as if they had no ideas either.
And I'd have to say that I think it's a sort of presumption
to expect the Holy Spirit to do on the day
something that I couldn't be bothered to do before the day.

Preaching the Gospel isn't an off-the-cuff improvisation.
It's what Jesus says it is: it's putting into words
what fills the heart. That's the key to it.

You can tell very easily when the homework has been done.
Listen to Cardinal Hume speaking without notes –
or a priest like Michael Hollings – and you realise that,
though there may be nothing written, there has in fact
been a great deal of preparation, a lifetime of preparation.

And that is what Our Lord is getting at.
The factor that links preachers like the Cardinal and
Fr Michael with the Jesuits in the Tower of London,
Edmund Campion and Robert Southwell, is that
they all speak from full hearts and well-furnished minds.
And that is essential in preaching the Gospel.
Prayer is raising one's own mind and heart to God;
preaching is raising other people's minds and hearts to God.

I write everything because I like to pray with a pen in my hand.
The very act of holding the pen channels the thoughts.

As I try to find the best way of expressing what is
in my mind and heart, the thoughts propel the pen
and the ideas find expression.
It's very often a good tactic to jot things down as you pray.

I learnt from a long-dead Victorian headmaster, Edward Thring,
whose sermons I studied, that one needs to start to think
about next Sunday's sermon on Monday morning –
to look at the text and let it reverberate all week,
and then on Friday or Saturday, try to distil the essence
of the thinking, pen in hand.

I also learnt from my years in the BBC
that no-one writes a good script straight off.
It needs to be honed, and recast,
and rewritten until there is maximum clarity.

So a Victorian Anglican, and the techniques
of twentieth-century broadcasting, point in the same direction.
First, think; then write, to crystallise thought;
then rethink, to edit what has been written.

It's not an original idea really.
St Ignatius of Loyola used to say:
'Work as if everything depended on you,
and then pray as if everything depended on God.'
When Jesus urges me to trust the Holy Spirit,
I don't presume he'll save me from doing my homework;
I assume that, if I put in the effort,
he'll speak through my work.

During the week it's my job to clear my mind
and fill my heart with the Gospel, because on Sundays
you will be able to discern whether or not
the words flow out of what is in my heart.

For priests, preaching the Gospel is the purpose
of their lives – not just in the words of sermons,
but in the body language of their whole lives.

And I'm saying all this to you because it relates to you too.
You also have to preach the Gospel in the world around you,
and you can't rely on finding the right words
if you don't put in the preparation.

It is the thinking of the mind and the exercise of the heart
during the week that leads to the Sunday sermon,
not just for me, but for you too.

A man's words flow from what fills his heart.

Chapter 3

Go and sell everything that you own . . .

When my uncle Gerald was a little lad of about seven or eight he was dead keen on marbles. He loved playing marbles in the street. He and his pals would take their marbles out and roll them along the pavement – more interesting than on grass – or indoors, because of the unexpected obstacles. And one day the obstacles included a rather large puddle. It was right in the way, and he didn't want to roll his marbles through the water, so what did he do? He took his trousers off and used them to mop up the puddle so he could play through. Obvious!

It wasn't all that obvious to his mother, but then she was a rather conventional woman who thought clean pants were more important than a game of marbles. It's all a question of priorities, really.

I remembered that episode when I first heard the story of Francis. He was a young man who realised that his family's wealth had been accumulated by his father's business deals. His father was a merchant who traded in cloth. But to manufacture those brilliant cloths many poor people were paid a pittance and were contaminated by the chemicals and the dyes. Francis decided he didn't want to inherit wealth that came from such a trade. He decided he'd work for the poor and, when his father objected, Francis took off all his rich clothes and stood there naked just as God made him. He quit the family home in Assisi and went off to live a life of complete poverty, loving God and serving the poor. It's all a question of priorities.

The problem with fine clothes is that they get to matter too much; they get in the way of the person underneath.

My uncle Gerald decided that mopping up a puddle was more important than looking smart. Francis of Assisi decided that fine clothes were an abuse of the poor.

We become so intent on designer labels, special T-shirts, special trainers that we forget other values. Do we really need so *many* clothes? Do they *have* to cost so much?

We can all laugh when we read about Imelda Marcos and her cupboards full of thousands of shoes – bizarre! But don't we have more than we need?
We can all gasp at the amount of money Princess Diana spent on her dresses, and then remember that, after using them to strengthen her public image, she sold them to raise money for her charities. Would we be able to part with our possessions like that?

The rich young man in today's Gospel was a decent young fellow. He did a lot of good; he wasn't a tear-away. And he vaguely thought he'd like to use his life for good causes. But to do that properly, he had to give up the high life, and he couldn't bring himself to give up his possessions. He went away sad because he realised that the fulfilment he longed for could only be his if he wasn't tied to his possessions. His possessions owned him.

There's nothing wrong in owning things, until they own us and control our lives. When we become obsessed with what we want to own we are prisoners of our possessions. We get to the point when we value clothes, fashion, cars, mountain bikes, foreign trips, stereos more than we value people. And at that point we cease to be Christians. People matter. Possessions don't matter, clothes don't matter. That's the whole point about possessions. If we use them for the benefit of others there's no harm in them. But when we begin to think more about our clothes, our cars, than we think about people, we're lost.

The young man in the Gospel couldn't bear the thought of losing his wealth, and went off to a sad and lonely life, rich in possessions, but impoverished in love.

St Francis gave up every single thing he had and found fulfilment in loving everyone as his brothers and sisters.

It's all a matter of priorities.

The faith on a hill-top

The Rock of Cashel commands a wide plain on the road from Dublin to Cork and was for centuries a fortress. Patrick came there in 450 and baptized King Aengus. The next four kings were either bishop or hermit or abbot as well as secular rulers. Four centuries later St Cormac was also both King of Munster and Bishop of Cashel. He was born about 837 and compiled the still extant Psalter of Cashel. He died in battle in 908. Two centuries after that, Cashel was granted to the Church and another Cormac, MacCarthach, Bishop and King of Desmond, founded the beautiful gem of Romanesque architecture known as Cormac's Chapel and consecrated it in 1134.

Chapter 4

Christ the King

My grandfather was born in County Leitrim,
in the little town of Drumshanbo.

He went to school a mile or two outside the town,
out on the Dowra Road, on the shores of Lough Allen.
On the far side the open-cast coal mines of Arrigna,
on this side the long gaunt slopes of Slieve an Ireann.

On Sundays he'd walk into the town to Mass,
carrying his shoes tied by their laces round his neck
till he came to the bridge below the town,
and there he'd stop and put on his boots
and walk up to Mass all respectable.

The Church is on the hill, but the road that leads up to it
is called Convent Avenue because next door to the church
is the Franciscan Convent of Our Lady of the Angels.

I went to Drumshanbo for the first time when I was seven
and understood why Grandad had been so sad to leave it
and why my Mother went there every peacetime year of her life
till she was ninety.

It hasn't the grandeur of Kerry or Donegal but it has its own
gentle beauty. And up there on the hill are the five acres
given to the nuns in 1863 by Hugh O'Beirne of Drumsna.

The first High Mass was said in the Convent on the Feast
of the Immaculate Conception in 1864. Five years later,
on 11 September 1869, while the nuns were in chapel at Mass,

> 'A bright light, whiter and clearer than that usually produced
> by the sun, appeared on the left side of the ceiling.

'At first it flickered with great rapidity but confined itself
to that particular spot. Gradually, as the Mass went on,
the bright light took the form of a Cross about two
and a half feet long, with the arms in proportion.

'On the Cross was attached a Heart larger than a human heart
of ordinary size. This also was formed of light –
not a simple outline but full, and as if raised and
full of animation, beating and throbbing against the Cross,
to which it seemed attached.

'The apparition lasted about eight minutes, or rather more,
from the time it took the distinct form,
and then dissolved gradually in a few seconds'.

It was seen by the Mother Abbess and three other nuns.
It reappeared two days later, and was perfect at the end of Mass
when Exposition of the Blessed Sacrament began.

The nuns could find no natural explanation for it
and interpreted it as a blessing on their wish to
make the Exposition and Perpetual Adoration
of the Blessed Sacrament their central observance.

Bishop McCabe took their wish to Pope Pius IX
in Rome at the beginning of 1870 and he approved it,
not just as a special devotion, but as part of their Rule.
So, on the feast of the Annunciation that Spring,
on 25 March, there started the perpetual Adoration
by day and night which has gone on from that day to this.

In that little convent on a bleak hill of Leitrim,
the Eucharistic King was enthroned and is enthroned still.

When we talk of kings we use the language of furniture
to symbolise their power.

A king is solemnly enthroned and the throne itself –
in the House of Lords, for example – speaks of the
dominant role of the monarch.

And so it is an eloquent gesture which recognises the
Kingship of Christ when we enthrone him sacramentally.
In this church we do it twice each weekend,
on Saturday morning, between Masses,
and on Sunday evening at Benediction.
Christ the King emerges from the Tabernacle and takes
his seat before our eyes, solemnly enthroned on the altar.

And in a few wonderfully privileged places,
that enthroning of the Blessed Sacrament is a continuous,
never-ending perpetual adoration of Christ the King.
In our own diocese the Benedictine nuns
at the martyrs' shrine at Tyburn keep a twenty-four-hour watch
before the Blessed Sacrament, ensuring
that not for an instant in any day is Christ neglected.
But whenever I celebrate the feast of Christ the King,
my mind goes to the top of the hill overlooking
Slieve an Ireann and Lough Allen, where the
present-day followers of St Francis and St Clare
form the court of the Eucharistic King.

Chapter 5

He remained there forty days.

Doing what? Enduring temptations? Yes.
Fasting? Yes. But, first and foremost, praying. Yes.
That was his prime purpose: to find a lonely place,
free from distractions, so he could focus on God
and communicate with his Father.
Earth is full of distractions, and temptations.
We all know that, and we all understand the need
to get away from it all and go to the sun,
take a break, to refresh ourselves.

That's what holidays are for, and on St Patrick's Day each year
I find myself longing for my next sight of Croagh Patrick,
and the twelve Bens, and Hungry Hill and Slieve an Ireann.
To get away from the humdrum and the everyday, and to
lift up our eyes to the hills from whence comes our help.
Yes, we can understand that. But, hang on a minute;
the forty days of fasting in the wilderness wasn't quite a
Saga holiday. It was a very different sort of experience.
The time Jesus spent in the desert wasn't a restorative
break: it wasn't even a calming retreat. It was a time apart
and, as we know, you can't escape temptation, even during
a time apart. If anything, the Devil redoubles his efforts
to shatter our serenity when he has a clear field.
As soon as we clear our thoughts to pray,
the Devil pops in his distractions and his temptations.

Jesus himself was faced with such distractions.
The Devil challenged him to throw himself down from the
temple roof, knowing that angels would fly to his rescue.
The sarcastic mob below the Cross on Calvary invited

him to use his power to come down from the Cross.
Whether he was caught up in the traumas of Good Friday
or apparently taking time out in the peace of the desert,
there was no stage in his human life when Jesus
was not subject to the temptations that beset us all.

His entire life was the making of selfless choices –
rejecting the temptations, accepting the consequences
of genuine Love. And what helped him to make those
hard choices was his awareness of the Father with him, and
that is why he spent time apart. Not to escape from people;
not even to avoid temptations, but simply to be
with his Father, to be in touch with the eternal,
to raise his mind and heart to God – in other words, to pray.
And, in that, we need to follow him. We need to set
time aside, we need to distance ourselves from the everyday
in order to bring God back into the centre of our life,
into our heart of hearts.

It is a deep human need to create time apart to enable ourselves
fully to open our hearts to God and to listen to whatever
he wishes to say.

It's not a time for thinking as such, but for clearing the mind.
It's not a time for formulas of prayer but for listening.
It's not a time for going deep into oneself,
but for leaving one's self behind.

More often than not, I find it when listening to music;
but that's not the only way, even for me.
I find it too among the hills which I mentioned earlier.
I find it in the Chilterns and on the road to Stratford.
I find it in an empty church that is suddenly filled to the brim
with the silent love of God.
I find it at Mass when the unseen congregation of saints
joins the visible congregation in the church.

I find it when my fingers pass over the rosary beads in my pocket
when I'm waiting for a train.
I find it because, for a short time or a longer period,
I have gone to find it – a place and a time set apart.

It's not *saying* prayers: it's *being open* to responses.
It's not bothering God with my problems; it's hearing
what he wants to say. It's not words I'm trying to find,
it's the words that come unbidden into my mind.

What does all this mean in practical terms? That it is
good for all of us during these forty days of Lent to seek
the chance to pray, to find a place apart, to set time aside,
to be in the presence of God. Don't bother about what
you're going to say to him: simply go into his presence
and be still, and listen to whatever it is He wants to put
into your mind.

Chapter 6

The men in the boat bowed down before him
and said, 'Truly you are the Son of God'.

I want to think about the Mass and how we value it.

We're aware that what the priest is doing
was set by Jesus himself at the Last Supper.
On the night before he died, he gathered his disciples
round him for what they only later realised was
the most significant meal of their lives.

For one of them – Judas – it was a meal of shame.
'One of you dipping into the dish with me will betray me.'

I remember as a child thinking how awful it was
that someone who intended to betray Jesus to such
a terrible death would first come to his party
and accept his hospitality – and kiss him
with such treachery in his heart.

That sense of horror at betrayal has never left me.
But for the other eleven, it was a puzzling meal.
It gathered them together – but it is only hindsight
that gives it its name: they didn't realise then
that it was 'the Last Supper'.

So one aspect of the Mass is the gathering,
being aware that we too are guests of Jesus,
and that he and we break bread together
as friends and allies, for mutual support and love.

And that aspect of the Mass is very important:
the shared meal. It's why we sometimes refer to
'the table of the Lord'. It's why we see
the breaking of bread as a shared experience.

It's why receiving Communion is dear to our hearts,
and it's why we share the experience
with our children at an early age.
Children need nourishing and Holy Communion
is the great proclamation of God feeding his children
with the bread of life.

It also explains why, during the week,
I take Communion to those unable to get to Mass.
It is a beautiful aspect of the sacramental outreach
of the Church that when someone can't come to God,
God comes to them.

This whole understanding of Communion is
essential to our spiritual growth.
When the devotion of the First Fridays was fostered,
it spoke of receiving Communion on nine successive
First Fridays – not just coming to Mass,
but receiving Communion.
So someone in hospital, for example, who can't get to Mass,
can still make the Nine Fridays.

At Communion we recall the Supper at which Jesus
gathered together his well-intentioned
but not always dependable disciples to give them food,
to give them strength for their life's journey.

As a meal, as a nourishing, the meaning of Communion
is very clear; and if that were all, it would still be tremendous.
But, in fact, it's NOT all and it is crucial that we don't stop there.
If that *were* all, then a Communion Service
would be just as good as a Mass. But the truth is greater still,
and it is infinitely more important to be present at Mass
than to receive Holy Communion outside Mass.

Yes, it *is* good to gather round the Lord's table
and accept his hospitality and be the better for it.

But that's how it affects *us* and we need to look
beyond ourselves and see the presence of God among us.

Just dwell on that phrase: God among us; *Dieu parmi nous.*
Christ didn't say 'This is a symbol of my presence.'
He said, 'This is my body which will be given up for you.'
'This is the cup of my blood, the blood of the new
and everlasting covenant. It will be shed for you
and for all so that sins may be forgiven.
Do this in memory of me.'

He was taking them into the heart of his mission,
into the meaning of his human existence.
Here is the Son of God come down to earth and
offering a sacrifice to his Father – the ultimate sacrifice
of his own life. That moment of time when Jesus died
on Calvary is the visible moment of the eternal sacrifice,
the ultimate expression of the love within the Trinity.

At the Last Supper, Jesus was explaining what would happen:
my body which *will* be given up for you . . .
the blood which *will* be shed, so that sins may be forgiven.
This is the deepest meaning of the Mass.

The apostles who had apparently been gathered together
for a meal were in fact being invited to witness
the sacrifice of the Lamb of God: a sacrifice so perfect
in the totality of its giving that it would take away
the sins of the world.

The sublime Sacrifice of the Cross on Calvary
is the sacrifice of the Mass.
At this moment we are in the presence of God:
He makes present to us the ultimately perfect love within God

And so that is why our beautiful picture
of the table of the Lord pales into insignificance, as it were,

beside this deeper vision of the altar
on which the Lamb of God offers himself.

If we change the focus from ourselves to God
we see that the Mass is the moment when we in time
are enabled to tune in to the eternal and ongoing
and ever-present Love within the Trinity.

This happiness and joy of a shared meal is eclipsed
by an even greater truth.
If Communion were all, we would only need a table.
But it is the Holy Sacrifice of the Mass we offer.
We offer the holy and perfect Sacrifice,
and stand alongside Mary our Mother
and John our *alter ego,* and it is an altar of sacrifice.

This is the true meaning of the Mass.
It is the Son's total love for the Father.
We come into the presence, the Real Presence,
of the Son's undying death, his love for the Father,
his perfect sacrifice.

And when the words of Jesus are spoken
as Jesus spoke them, and the bread becomes himself
and he offers himself to the Father, we —
like the men in the boat — bow down before him
and say, 'Truly you are the Son of God.'

The Mass is, above all else, the supreme Act of Worship.

Chapter 7

I am the living bread.

I spoke last week about the Mass as the moment
when we are brought into the very heart of God.
I want to explore this a little further this week.

God is a limitless energy of Love
and the Three Persons who make up the One God
are the three aspects of that Love.

The Father, who loves;
the Son, who is the loved one;
and the Spirit who proceeds from
the eternal exchange of that Love.
At its deepest, Love is self-sacrifice, and the Son's
self-sacrifice found its historical expression on Calvary.

That is why the true centre of our faith
is not just love but sacrifice, and why the centre
of our worship is not only the communion table
of loving hospitality but, even more importantly,
the altar of self-sacrifice.

The Mass brings us both to the table at the Last Supper,
and to the altar on which the Lamb of God
offered himself in sacrifice.

The First Eucharistic Prayer – the old Roman Canon –
includes a most wonderful prayer
which moves me afresh no matter how often I hear it:

> 'Almighty God, we pray that your angel' – your angel,
> your own messenger to us, your own beloved Son –

'we pray that your angel may take this sacrifice
to your altar in heaven.'

We are referring there to the eternal offering of the
Son to the Father – which we then relate
to its actual place within time when Jesus, God-made-man,
enacted his sacrifice on the Cross, on Calvary.

Our prayer continues:

Then, as we receive from this altar the sacred body
and blood of your Son, let us be filled with
every grace and blessing.

And how do we receive it?
We receive it under the sacramental sign of the bread of life –
bread to nourish and *fill* us.

Jesus identifies himself with the living bread
which has come down from heaven.
Fed, nourished, *filled* by that bread, we are then filled
with every grace and blessing.

All the things we need, all the things we want,
all the things we long for – all spring from
that action of making Jesus part of us.

Just as bread becomes the strength of the one who eats it,
so Jesus, who is the bread of life, becomes the strength
of the one who eats Him.

We are sinners, but we know we have found forgiveness.
We are mortal, but we know we have immortal souls.
We are limited by our earthly life, but we know we have
a limitless capacity for love when we become part of God,
and when God becomes part of us.

Let us be filled with every grace and blessing.

The key word is 'filled'.
We are no longer starving, we are filled.
We are no longer incomplete, we are fulfilled.
The completeness of our happiness comes from being fulfilled,
and *that* happens through the grace of God.

The Israelites, weak with hunger in the desert,
were filled with the manna which fell from heaven,
saved from hunger in this world.

But we who receive the bread of life, Jesus himself,
are saved, not only from hunger, but from death.

> Your fathers ate the manna in the desert, and they are dead;
> but this is the bread that comes down from heaven so that
> a man may eat it and not die.

The Third Eucharistic Prayer sets it out so simply and strongly:

> We offer you in thanksgiving this holy and living sacrifice.
> Look with favour on your Church's offering and see
> the Victim whose death has reconciled us to yourself.
> Grant that we, who are nourished by his body and blood
> may be filled with his Holy Spirit and become one body,
> one spirit in Christ.

That fulfilment of all our potential, that filling with the
Holy Spirit, that being filled with every grace and blessing,
comes to us through the Mass.

Here, in this living sacrifice of praise we are freed
from the corruption of sin and death. And therefore,
as the Fourth Eucharistic Prayer proclaims:

> We shall sing your glory with every creature through
> Christ Our Lord through whom you give us everything
> that is good.

It really is as simple and as wonderful as that.
Through the nourishing of our lives by Christ Our Lord,
we are indeed given everything that is good.

The Mass is the bridge from here to eternity.

I am the living bread.
Anyone who eats this bread will live for ever.

Chapter 8

Whoever eats me will draw life from me.

When we eat bread it becomes part of
our bodily chemistry and gives us strength.
When we eat the Bread of Life – Jesus –
He becomes part of our spiritual chemistry
and gives us strength.
So it is clearly in our best interests
to be regular communicants.
Whoever eats me will draw life from me.

We know that, at the Last Supper, Jesus broke the bread
and handed it round to his somewhat mystified friends.
They didn't really know what to make of it.
It wasn't till after Good Friday, after Easter,
that they were able to begin to explore
the huge reservoir of spiritual perceptions piled up
behind that idea of Jesus being the Bread of Life.

In those earliest days it probably seemed
no more than a sort of communion bread.
Their mood was no doubt solemn, but their
understanding was only just beginning to blossom.
Slowly but surely, the Church learnt to appreciate
the presence of Christ at every celebration
of the Lord's Supper.

One of the best indications of that was when the
Church realised that the Eucharist was for *all* the faithful –
not just the faithful present, but the suffering faithful,
absent because in prison for their faith.

Surely if Jesus wanted to be present to the faithful,
gathered together, he would want even more
to be present to those in prison.

And so the practice grew of preserving some
of the consecrated bread when Mass was over
so that it could be smuggled in to prisoners,
and later on taken to the sick and housebound.

At some moment in the fourth century
a young acolyte called Tarsicius was asked to take
the Blessed Sacrament to certain Christian prisoners.
With great love and reverence – and courage – he did so.
A young and dedicated extraordinary minister of the Eucharist.
But one day Tarsicius was intercepted by a hostile crowd.
He refused to hand over to them the precious gift
he was carrying and was bludgeoned to death.
His martyrdom speaks volumes about the reverence
Christians now felt for the Blessed Sacrament,
not only at Mass but at other times.

Between Masses, the Communion for the sick
was housed in special receptacles: hanging pyxes
and sacrament houses – the forerunners of our
present-day Tabernacle. I remember my Mother
explaining to me that, just as the Royal Standard
flying over Buckingham Palace told me that the
Queen was in residence, so the red lamp burning
before the Tabernacle told me that Christ the King
was in residence.

Within that Tabernacle is the real presence of Christ
in the Blessed Sacrament, still looking like bread,
but in substance transformed into Jesus:
body, blood, soul and divinity.

The Church's understanding had matured: the penny
had dropped that here is the presence of Jesus.
It's why we genuflect when we take our place in church;
it's why we bend the knee again when we leave.
Whenever we cross in front of the royal residence,
where the Lord is, we genuflect to him.

Why? I asked my Mother. Why do I have to genuflect
to him if I can't see him? Because, said my Mother,
because even if you can't see him, he's there and
he can see you. I wish all children were taught to be
so polite to Jesus in the Tabernacle.

Of course there are several practical problems relating
to the Blessed Sacrament, and particularly to the chalice.
If it were only blessed wine it would be no big deal
if it were accidentally spilled. But if it is truly the Blood of Christ,
then infinite care must be taken to avoid spillage.

As more and more people in larger and larger churches
came to Communion, that danger of spilling increased
and so eventually the Church drew back from offering
the chalice to everyone. And that seemed particularly sensible
in the last century when St Pius X welcomed children
of seven and eight to make their First Communion.

Another practical problem with the chalice is that
wine goes off. I remember a most embarrassing
experience at a Catholic school. I was asked to
consecrate enough wine for all to receive under both
kinds. But when I received from the chalice myself
I realised that the wine had been left uncorked and
was vinegar. I couldn't give that to the children,
nor could I simply throw it away, and so I had to
consume it all myself – a very full chalice of vinegar
which left me feeling ill for a couple of days.

And of course there is also the matter of hygiene –
sharing a cup is not always the wisest thing to do,
and when Sars became a problem in the Far East,
many who had received from the chalice before,
no longer did so. That's no problem, theologically.
When you receive the consecrated host you receive
the fullness of Christ – body, blood, soul and divinity.
It does not diminish the Sacrament in any way
to receive only the host.

For some people the problem is the other way round;
people allergic to wheat have to avoid bread, and
so either they can use special celiac hosts, as the
late Archbishop Derek Worlock had to do,
or they can come forward to receive only from the chalice.

Again, no problem, theologically: whoever receives
from the chalice receives exactly the same
divine person as the one who receives the host.
It is Jesus himself who enters our innermost being
and seats himself in the throne of our heart.
What matters is to recognise the Lord in
the breaking of bread and to receive him
with the greatest love and reverence.

Parents must explain it carefully to children.
When we come forward to receive Our Lord
in Communion, in the hand or on the tongue,
it is the most sacred moment of that day.
It is the moment when I reach out and welcome
Jesus into my heart and hear him say,

'Whoever eats me will draw life from me.'

Chapter 9

The worship they offer me is worthless;
the doctrines they teach are only human regulations.

Here is Jesus dealing with one of the recurring problems
in the history of religion: how can we be sure that
what we are doing is really pleasing to God?

The very word 'Pharisee' has come into the English language
to mean the supercilious and judgmental sort of person who
has 'pretensions to superior sanctity'.

The Pharisees emerged about a century before the birth
of Jesus and gradually formed a major pressure group.
The Hebrew word 'Pharisees' means 'the separated ones',
and that notion of being a people set apart
was both their strength and their downfall.

They are sometimes portrayed as great sticklers for the
letter of the law, but that's an unfair caricature.
The real fanatics were the Sadducees who tried
to apply the Law of Moses with total inflexibility.
The Pharisees were actually less rigid – more willing usually
to tailor the rules to different circumstances.

But on this particular occasion reported by St Mark
it was indeed the Pharisees who were getting uptight
about the failure of the disciples to wash their hands.
It's easy for us to see the danger. The Pharisees were forgetting that
it's not cleanliness of hands that really matters but cleanliness of heart.

It is indeed 'pharisaical' to observe all the rules and regulations
about ritual cleansing and not to be too bothered
about defaming people, defrauding them and
leading rich and exploitative lives.

41

Dickens didn't call it 'pharisaical' – he called it 'Humbug'.
It's an ongoing problem. Every truly Christian person
has to avoid becoming a Humbug.

I sometimes reflect on this after Communion,
when I'm cleansing the chalice.
I drain the last drops of the Precious Blood
and then water is poured in and swirled round
and then drunk to make absolutely sure that
the Blood is completely consumed.

It's not a great ceremony but it is deliberately
and prayerfully done in order to convey
the significance of what is there.

For you in the congregation it is a time of thanksgiving.
You have just received Jesus in the Blessed Sacrament
and you kneel there cherishing his presence in your hearts,
and your prayers go in parallel with the prayer of the priest.

And what am I saying while I am rinsing
and drying the chalice?
Silently, in my heart, the prayer is this:
'Lord, may I receive these gifts in purity of heart.
May they bring me healing and strength now and for ever.'

And that's the point of it. It's not so much the chalice
that needs to be purified, but me.
And that physical action of cleansing is the prompt to say:
make me clean. 'Lord give me purity of heart'.

I am particularly conscious of my chalice.
It was my Mother's gift to me at my ordination,
and after her death I fulfilled a promise that I would
attach her wedding ring to the base of the chalice.
I touch it every time I say Mass.

It is an inanimate object but made precious by its purpose.
Cleansing it takes only a few moments

but the prayer that accompanies it is an offering of the heart.
The object itself and the cleansing of it have value
only in what they prompt me to do and to be.

The things I have to deal with in my life are,
as Jesus said, the things that well up within me:
the greed, the jealousy, the selfishness;
and it's those that need cleansing out.

So that little interlude after communion, the cleansing
of the chalice, is not an episode of pharisaical ritual
but a nudge towards the real purpose –
a prayer for a cleansing of the heart.

That little job of washing-up becomes an offering of thanks
for a mother's love and for a Saviour's gift of himself.
In the world of the spirit it's such details that really matter.
Look after the spiritual pence
and the pounds will look after themselves.

It's *The Little Way* that leads to heaven.
Take each moment as it comes, each prayer,
each action, and value it not for itself
but for the way it keeps the heart on course.

Every action needs to be an act of love.
The worship we offer God must not be worthless,
but true love; the doctrines we teach must
not be human regulations but the strategies of love.

Next Wednesday, we'll be celebrating the feast of
St Gregory the Great, the first pope to have been a monk,
the Bishop of Rome who sent the monk Augustine
to bring Christianity to England.
And Gregory was aware of his own need to purify his heart,
and to match words and deeds.

I like to imagine him cleansing his chalice
at the end of his Mass – not content just to be doing

the right thing in the correct way
but reflecting on his own need to be cleansed.

Gregory admitted his failures:
'When I lived in a monastic community
I was able to keep my tongue from idle topics and
to devote my mind almost continually to the
discipline of prayer. Since taking on my shoulders
the burden of pastoral care I have been unable
to keep steadily recollected because my mind
is distracted by many responsibilities.'

Doesn't that ring true? For all of us?
So many distractions? Unable to keep recollected?

But Gregory saw how God might use that:
'I do not stand on the pinnacle of achievement', he said,
'I languish rather in the depths of my weakness.
And yet the creator and redeemer of mankind can give me,
unworthy though I be, the grace to see life whole,
and power to speak effectively of it. It is for love of him
that I do not spare myself in preaching him.'

No humbug there. No Pharisee. Gregory was the first pope
to call himself 'the servant of the servants of God'.
We can identify with him.

As I cleanse the chalice,
and as you kneel in thanksgiving and see that cleansing going on,
we can all make Gregory's prayer our own:

> Lord, purify us and give us the grace to see life whole
> and power to speak effectively about it.

Chapter 10

It was very early on the first day of the week, and still dark,
when Mary of Magdala came to the tomb . . .

I remember this morning, Easter Sunday, 1969.

It was the morning my father died. He had been ill for
several months and in hospital, but came home at weekends.
He couldn't be left on his own.

On that Easter Sunday my mother and I tossed for which
of us would go to the early Mass and which to the later.
It was while she was at the early Mass and I was at home
with him that he collapsed and died.

If you ask me what happened, I would be able to tell you
quite a lot, though it was such a shock that I may well
misremember things.

If you ask my mother what happened, she would have to
start from driving back from Mass and seeing an ambulance
outside the house, and I daresay shock would make some
of her recollection rather unreliable too.

We were the main participants, but we would highlight
different things and might even contradict one another.
But then it is twenty-six years ago and my mother is very
old and frail and I know I just can't remember some details.
But though the versions might differ, the one certain fact is
that he died on Easter Sunday morning, twenty-six years ago.

The Gospel we heard this morning was derived from John
the beloved disciple, a participant; and whether he wrote it
himself, or it came through one of his own followers,
it's the strong memory of one who was there.

But of course all he really remembered
was how the event affected him.

John said Mary of Magdala came 'while it was still dark'
but Luke says it was 'at the first sign of dawn'.
Mark says it was 'just as the sun was rising'.
Matthew says – like John – it was 'towards dawn'.

John's recollection was that he was with Peter when
Mary came running up to them and then he raced off
with Peter to see for themselves. Luke, on the other
hand, probably had the story from the women – and
it's a fuller story. It wasn't just Mary of Magdala,
but Joanna too, and Mary the mother of James, and
others. As they remembered it, they were standing
bewildered by the empty tomb when two men appeared
to them in brilliant clothes and said,
'He is not here; he is risen.'

Matthew's version has the stone rolled back
as part of an earthquake, and an angel – one angel –
appeared not only to the women, but to the
terror-stricken Roman guards.

Not surprising that there should be conflicting memories.
These were documents written at least twenty to thirty
years after the event so some discrepancies are inevitable.
But it doesn't affect the central truth at all.

Just as my memory and my mother's memory of Easter '69
are different and even contradictory, so the Gospel memories
of the First Easter are different and even contradictory.

What Mother and I agree on, is that on that morning,
suddenly, death came to my father.
What the four Gospels agree on is that, on that morning,

life eternal came to humanity through the resurrection of Christ. The one inescapable fact is: he is not here; he is risen.

A man whose sufferings caused him to die long before the two thieves executed with him; a man whose lifeblood had totally drained from his body; a man whose corpse had been placed under guard to prevent fraud. That man came back to life and that is the great truth of the resurrection.

Paul spelt out its implications: Christ, having been raised from the dead, will never die again. John went into the empty tomb and for the first time realised what it meant: that he must rise from the dead.

For Christ, death is an enemy now vanquished, and for Christians destined to follow Christ, the way lies open to resurrection and eternal life. It leaves us with the exultant faith in a Christ who lives now, eternally lives and beckons us to eternal life.

> Let him easter in us,
> be a dayspring to the dimness of us,
> be a crimson-cresseted east.

The sunrise on Easter Sunday is not just one more daybreak, but a new experience bridging time and eternity. Christ, the Morning Star, who came back from the dead and shed his peaceful light on all mankind, is sitting now on the right hand of God and is calling us through death to life.

When we thought about it afterwards we both of us realised how great a privilege it was for death to come to my father during the Easter-morning Mass.

Christ, my hope, has risen; he goes before you into Galilee. In the words of the great Anglo-Saxon poem, *The Dream of the Rood:*

He loosed us from bondage and life he gave to us
And a home in Heaven. Hope sprang up again
Bright with blessing to those burning in pain.
Christ the Son of God journeyed as a conqueror,
Mighty and victorious, when with many in his train,
A great company of souls, he came to God's Kingdom.

Chapter 11

Anyone who is not against us is for us.

It's the easiest thing in the world to be partisan.

On the first of his several amazing voyages, Lemuel Gulliver was shipwrecked on the shores of the empire of Lilliput, an island populated to his astonishment by people no taller than your finger. Gulliver soon discovered that the neighbouring empires of Lilliput and Blefuscu had been at daggers drawn for many moons.

It all began upon the following occasion:

'It is allowed on all hands that the primitive way of breaking eggs before we eat them was upon the larger end. But his present Majesty's grandfather while he was a boy, going to eat an egg and breaking it according to the ancient practice, happened to cut one of his fingers. Whereupon the Emperor, his father, published an edict commanding all his subjects, upon great penalties, to break the smaller end of their egg.

'The people so highly resented this law that our histories tell us there have been six rebellions raised on that account, wherein one Emperor lost his life and another his crown. These civil commotions were constantly fomented by the monarchs of Blefuscu; and when they were quelled, the exiles always fled for refuge to that empire. It is computed that eleven thousand persons have, at several times, suffered death rather than submit to break their eggs at the smaller end. Many hundred large volumes have been published upon this controversy. But the books of the Big-Endians have been long forbidden, and the whole party rendered incapable by law of holding employments.

'During the course of these troubles, the Emperors of Blefuscu did frequently expostulate by their ambassadors, accusing us of making a schism in religion by offending against a fundamental doctrine of our great prophet Lustrog, in the 54th Chapter of the Blundeeral (which is their Alcoran). This, however, is thought to be a mere strain upon the text. For the words are these: that all true believers shall break their eggs at the convenient end; and which *is* the convenient end seems, in my humble opinion, to be left to every man's conscience . . .'

Thus, in *Gulliver's Travels,* did Dean Swift satirize some of the dafter divisions within Christianity and the ferocity with which Christians love to exclude one another.

To non-Christians it is simply incredible that creatures of the same God should be so persistently antagonistic to one another.

'Come to me, you who are overburdened,' says Jesus.

'I will leave the ninety-nine to go in search of the one who is lost', says Jesus.

'Father, forgive them' says Jesus, looking at every single human being.

Yet we persist in thinking that it is the task of the Church to rule people out. And that temptation to exclude recurs with sickening frequency in the history of religion.

Eldad and Medad didn't go to the Tent as they should have done, but prophesied anyway; and there's Joshua indignantly delating them: 'My Lord Moses, stop them.'

And then there's John complaining to Jesus that someone who – in Mrs Thatcher's chilling phrase – was not one of us, was using the name of Jesus to cast out devils 'so we tried to stop them'. You can hear how disappointed Jesus is, 'You mustn't stop him. Anyone who is not against us,

is for us.' The difference between John and Jesus is the difference between being sectarian and being Catholic.
Sectarians by and large exclude others.
Catholics by and large *in*clude others.

It is sectarian to search out whatever divides people and make an issue of it. It is Catholic to proclaim what unites people and make a virtue of it. Between these two outlooks on the world there is a vast gulf. On the one hand the complacent satisfaction with self, the narrow-minded, the excluding.
On the other hand, a determination to seek deeper wisdom, a mind and heart open to new insights, an inclusive approach to all mankind.

I am reminded of an address given to the Teachers' Guild in 1887 by my great hero Edward Thring. 'Earth', he said bluntly, 'is a battlefield. The clash of armies meeting is a mere transient symptom of the ceaseless strife that ebbs and flows all unperceived in every city, village, home, nay in every human heart. Mankind is divided into two camps. There are the lordly spirits who look on the world as subject to their power, and take the scissors of creation into their hands, and proceed to cut the universe into little squares. This is one camp, the camp of intellect and knowledge.

'Then there are the Shakespeares and all those pupils of light who approach infinity with eyes open and loving and humble. This is the other camp, the camp of the seeing heart and the seeing eye.'

Just think of our own society now: we know so much, and how to do so much, but we don't know *why* we do it. We can make babies in test tubes; we can genetically modify crops; we can send a rocket to Jupiter; but we lack the wisdom to use that knowledge.
Knowledge comes but wisdom lingers.

Those who see the world as a market place act on the competitive principle that anyone who is not with us must be against us.

Those who see the world as the Kingdom of God act on the inclusive principle that anyone who is not against us is for us.

Chapter 12

Woman, why turn to me?

In all the turmoil that has engulfed our sacristy,
a piece of paper fluttered out of some dismantled cupboard –
a handbill for a Mission given here in 1949 –
and I've put it on the table here and when you've seen it
I'll hand it over to our archivist.

It's a handbill, and I imagine copies were shoved
through every letterbox in Ruislip by the
Legion of Mary and other long-forgotten good people.
'Christianity' – it says boldly at the top:
'Christianity offers the only SURE ANSWER to
All Your Problems. Come to the Mission.'

Good Lord, I thought: what a splendidly confident thing to say.
If we were putting out a handbill like that today
we'd be awfully mealy-mouthed.
We'd be asking, 'Catholicism – is it for you?'
We'd be venturing to suggest, 'Test-drive the Catholic Church –
see if it suits your temperament.'
Or, worst of all, we'd be saying: 'Have you got problems?
Brother, so have we in the Catholic Church, and ours
are worse than yours!!!'

What happened to that Catholic confidence of fifty years ago?
I remember when I was going through Allen Hall,
getting rather ratty with one of my fellow-students.
He had the misfortune to be 25 years younger than me!
He wasn't born till after Vatican II and he was telling me
how really awful the Church was before the Council.

With the sort of absolute infallibility that comes from
total ignorance, he told me that no-one ever read the Bible,
no-one could understand the Mass in Latin,
no-one dared contradict a priest (he'd never met my mother!)
no-one ever thought for himself.
The whole Church was run on fear
and the popes were triumphalist.

And he was really taken aback when I said 'Bunkum!'
If it was as awful as that I would have noticed.
If it was as terrible as that I couldn't have lived with it
during the years when in actual fact I was going to
daily Mass and deepening my love of the Church.

I said, 'You're talking total tosh.
The Catholics of 1950 loved the Church and the Mass
every bit as much as you, if not more.
The Catholics of 1950 worked their socks off
to build churches and schools.
How dare you be so snide about their faith?'

He was so startled at my ferocity that I thought
he was going to burst into tears.
I said, 'Look – there's never been a time when the
Church was perfect, but equally there's never been a
time when the Holy Spirit wasn't at work in the Church.
You seem to think that, between the age of the Apostles
and your own generation, the Holy Spirit was having a long nap.
That's theologically stupid as well as historically ignorant.'

The one thing a historian can *always* see in the
Catholic Church is confidence.
A confidence in the faith, in every generation.
Holiness, in every generation.
Love of God and neighbour, in every generation.
And in this generation we need to rediscover that confidence.

Too many Catholics these days are like
religious chameleons trying not to stand out
against an ecumenical background.
The faith isn't about how little you need to believe,
but how much you can give to the faith.
We belong to a Church which is the mystical body of Christ,
a Church which was launched by the Apostles and guided
in every generation by the successors of Peter.
Every age has had its own new problems,
and in every age the only sure answer has been in the Church.

It's the same today; all sorts of new problems: cloning,
respirators, AIDS, divorce, artificial insemination,
single parents, global warming, nuclear fission.
They all look new, but they are all variations on basic problems.
Jesus might not have had direct experience of global warming,
but he did live with super-powers trying to feed their greed
at the expense of the rest of the world.

The Gospel message, in its essentials, relates to all ages
and all situations and all problems.
The problem at Cana looks at first sight a fairly small one:
Who forgot to order the vino for the reception?
The real problem wasn't a shortage of plonk.
The real problem was the embarrassment
of two young people on their big day.
Jesus wasn't trying to be a one-man Oddbins.
He was doing all in his power to rescue two people from humiliation.

The message is: don't get too bothered
about setting the whole world to rights.
Just solve the immediate problem on your own doorstep.
'Woman, why turn to me,' he says.
And wisely, Mary doesn't say anything too clever back:
she's content *not* to spell it out.

Why turn to you?
Because you're the one who offers the only
SURE ANSWER to this problem.

It's still true in Ruislip in 1998.
It's been true for two thousand years: He's the only one
with a sure answer to whatever problem.
If you fall in love with Catholicism,
notwithstanding its wrinkles;
if you immerse yourself in the Gospel,
notwithstanding the silliness of some of its so-called supporters;
if you do actually try to commit every minute of your day
to trying to live like Christ, the problems are solved.
The problems don't vanish, but they do become
merely problems, and problems can be solved.

Let's just remind ourselves that, with faith, anything is possible.
With faith: *con fide* – it means with faith.
Confidence is being with faith.
Christianity offers the only SURE ANSWER to
All Your Problems.

That's cool – it does!

Chapter 13

We worked hard all night and caught nothing.

There's a deep satisfaction in the work of a wood-carver.
I've watched wood-carvers in Bavaria coax statues out of wood –
it's almost as if the image is hidden within the wood
and the craftsman knows how to release it.

When you make a plaster-cast statue
you get mass-production of soulless images, all identical.
And although painters try to animate the statue with colour,
the statues remain lifeless and boring.

I've seen so many statues of the Little Flower,
St Thérèse of Lisieux, standing po-faced and immobile,
a dead-eyed parody of holiness.
And then in Oberammergau I found a little statue of her
in which the Carmelite robes swirl and the skill of the carver
gives a semblance of vitality.

I'm not deluding myself. That too is mass-produced and
not to be compared with a one-off, a genuine carving
which you can identify as a uniquely beautiful creation.
There's no satisfaction in mass-producing stereotypes.
There is a much more genuine satisfaction
for the carver of the one-off;
to see something you have made is profoundly satisfying.

At the end of the day, the carver sweeps up the wood-shavings
and looks at his statue and sees a result.
Goodness, how we all long to see real results from our efforts.
At the end of a teacher's day there's no such result.
You hope you've transferred some ideas,

you hope you've made a few facts memorable,
you hope you've had some influence.
But you don't know and you probably won't ever know.
Only years afterwards, maybe, someone will come up to
you and say 'You won't remember me but you used to
teach me – and suddenly I realised what poetry was all about.'
Only then do you have any inkling
about what your work actually achieved.

And it's the same with the Gospel.
Being a Catholic isn't a matter of making plastic saints,
it's not even a matter of using skills to create more lively images,
it's not even a matter of an artist's vision
creating a one-off work of art –
it's a realisation of wisdom and inspiration.

We don't preach through the meaning of our words,
but through the integrity of our lives.
And that's something we ourselves can't measure.
Each of us knows we are supposed to win followers for Christ –
but it's not something we can see happening.
It's a matter of constancy, and patience, and tenacity,
and fidelity, and honesty – and all those literally take
years to have any effect.

What I *said* as a young man was pribble and prabble;
what I'm saying now as a nearing-retirement man is a
little better. But it's what I *do* consistently and faithfully
down the years that gives my words any value.

We find ourselves like Simon Peter working hard
all night and catching nothing.
And people get discouraged because they're doing
their best and nothing much seems to come of it.

But that's O.K. – that's the way it works.
I may live for a hundred years.

I may labour every day to do and say all the right things –
but of all the million words I offer, only one
will enter someone else's life and bring them to God.
Only one. It's not really surprising.

The only thing you remember about King Alfred
is that he burnt some cakes.
The only thing you remember about Geoff Hurst
is that they thought that it was all over, and it is now.
One moment, from a whole life!

We don't know, of all the minutes in our lives,
which will be the unforgettable one.
We don't know, of all the words we utter,
which will be the powerful one.
We don't know. But God does.

So don't be discouraged when your life
doesn't seem to have much to show for it.
If God wants to use us, he will.

We simply have to live our lives to the full and
give him as much as we can for him to choose from.

SITIO

Sitio. I thirst.

*Father Michael Hollings chose this image
by Philip Hagreen for his ordination card
and re-used it at the time of his jubilee.*

Chapter 14

Here we are preaching a crucified Christ.

The memory card given to the congregation in the Cathedral,
at the Requiem for Father Michael Hollings,
had a striking image of Our Lord on the Cross,
and underneath, the Latin word *Sitio,* I thirst.

The Cardinal said it was the image of the Crucifix that he saw
when he went to visit Fr Michael in intensive care.
His long life was a living sacrifice of himself.
His death, too, enabled him to identify his own suffering
with the suffering of Christ on the Cross.

Fr Michael came to be chaplain at Oxford at the start of my
second year there. When I first went up, I had dutifully
registered at the Chaplaincy but it seemed to exist mainly
for public school boys and I found no welcome there, and
opted for the local parish church of St Aloysius and went
to Mass every morning there. But when year two began
I went down to meet the new chaplain and found him a
completely different kettle of fish; a bit shy, but friendly
and warm, and curious, and good-humoured, and
lively-minded. No longer did one wait for formal invitations
to dine with the chaplain. Michael's door was always open
and people were fed and watered on an epic scale.

He had been a soldier in World War II and won the Military Cross.
He didn't lack courage. He knew what life and hardship could do
to people and he was impatient to help. The obituaries have spoken
about his great work for race relations when he moved on to Southall
and Bayswater, and his down-to-earth concern for the poor and the
disadvantaged. But he also took the Gospel seriously in another way.

He took entirely literally the Scriptural injunction
to pray without ceasing.

He understood the teaching of Jesus because he loved God
wholeheartedly, and constantly tried to put himself into
the presence of God. His strength came from his priesthood
and his whole life centred on the Mass.
He said Mass gently and thoughtfully;
his whole mind was concentrated on the living presence
of the crucified and risen Christ.

He murmured the prayers as if he was meeting them for the
first time and, when he elevated the Host after the consecration,
you could sense his awe before the Real Presence of God
among us. The Mass is God's coming to earth in love,
and when I think of Fr Michael, my first image of him
is of the priest offering the ultimate sacrifice of Calvary.

One of the great lessons he taught me was that time is the
most precious gift of God and you mustn't waste a moment of it.
He gave the appearance that he was always available, and he
could do that because he kept a tight diary and expanded his
day to meet the demands. He sat up long after midnight to listen
to people going through crises – and then he'd be up again long
before anyone else to make sure he had enough time to pray.
He painted himself into a corner deliberately – he preached
the necessity of starting every day with an hour or more
of prayer and therefore had to get on with it. It's a good tactic.
If you *say* you'll do something, you jolly well have to *do* it.

There might be one or more Masses in a day, prayer groups
and meetings, lots of prayers and spiritual activity with others
but every day had to start with him and God together,
he huddled in his great black cloak watching before the
Blessed Sacrament on his own. Not many were up at that hour
to see him. But for him it was essential: prayer and the Mass.

His whole priesthood was a painting himself into a corner.
He preached, therefore he did. I have never known anyone
who so totally practised what he preached. I didn't agree
with all his views; I couldn't have followed all his policies;
I wouldn't defend all his positions.

But his was a living priesthood, he was always there
when you needed him; and at other times he expected
you not to pester him so he could be free for others
when they needed him.

When I was ordained in 1988 he had recently had surgery
and couldn't process with the rest of the clergy,
but quietly took his place in the sanctuary before the
Mass started. That meant that, when I approached the
altar towards the very front of the procession, the only
priest already in the sanctuary was Michael Hollings.
He was there not just to support me, but to welcome me.

After eleven tremendous years at Oxford he was Parish Priest
at Southall, and then nineteen years in Bayswater
where, last Friday night, a West Indian steel band was
on hand to play in his honour after a Requiem there.
His dying was difficult, much pain and suffering,
following on a terrible episode of slanderous assault
on his good name. He was in intensive care at
St Mary's, Paddington: a leg was amputated.
The suffering enabled him to identify once again
with the Christ he had served all his life.

It's never easy to lead a Christian life, but if you've
painted yourself into a corner by taking the name of
Christ then you have to embrace the way of the Cross.
After a talk with Michael, he'd invariably say, as you
left him: 'Courage! Press on.'

He would identify completely with St Paul writing to his converts at Philippi:

> I am no longer trying for perfection by my own efforts; I want only the perfection that comes through faith in Christ; and is from God, and based on faith. All I want is to know Christ and the power of his resurrection and to share his sufferings by reproducing the pattern of his death. All I can say is that I forget the past and I press on for what is still to come.

I thirst. Those who were hungry and thirsty he fed. Those who hungered and thirsted for God he fed.

May he rest in peace.

Chapter 15

These are the trials through which we triumph
by the power of him who loved us.

Sixty years ago this week, a woman in her early
fifties stepped into a gas chamber, as did so many
of her fellow-Jews. She'd been picked up a week
earlier in Holland and crammed into a cattle-truck
to take her to Auschwitz. What makes her unusual
among all those millions of victims is that at the
time of her death she was a Carmelite nun.

She was Edith Stein, the youngest of seven children
in a loving Jewish family in Breslau, in that part of Europe
so long disputed between Germany and Poland.
She was born on the great Jewish feast of the Atonement,
Yom Kippur, but her father died when she was only two,
leaving her mother to look after both his business and his family.

Edith was very bright indeed, strong of intellect and
strong of will. She read everything she could lay her
hands on and, like many a bright girl before and since,
enjoyed challenging conventional wisdom.
To her mother's bewilderment
she decided to leave school at fifteen,
in effect taking a gap year,
while living with her married sister in Hamburg.

It had the effect of making her value her studies all the more.
When she returned, she sailed through her exams
and headed towards a career in teaching.
Her main intellectual concern was philosophy,
and in due course she got her doctorate.

She was also rethinking her religious position.
She wandered into the cathedral at Frankfurt just
to look round and was intrigued to see an ordinary
housewife come in and put her basket down for a
few moments while she said some prayers.

So unlike the communal Jewish observance of the
Sabbath, here was someone just popping into church
while it was empty, in the middle of her shopping,
as if to have a quick chat with a friend.

Edith never forgot that insight into the way
that Catholics enter into conversation with God.
She got herself a Missal and went to Mass,
and in due course she was baptised. For a time
she taught at a Dominican convent, and then
at the University of Münster. But the call
of the cloister was getting stronger and stronger –
the need to centre her whole life in prayer and
the praise of God.

She was forty-two when she entered Carmel
in Cologne and became Teresa Benedicta of the Cross.
Why Teresa? She'd read the autobiography
of St Teresa of Avila – like herself, a woman who was both
wonderfully down to earth and very close to God.

It was the period of the rise of Hitler in Germany,
and terrible anti-Semitism. Hatred of the Jews
was part of the Nazi mind-set, and long before
the war, Jews in Germany and then Austria felt
increasingly in danger. I remember several much-
respected senior colleagues in the BBC who had
in the 'thirties realised that there was no future
for them in Germany and had made new lives for
themselves here.

Unfortunately, the British government and several others were more concerned to appease Hitler than to oppose him. The only outright condemnation came from the Vatican. Pope Pius XI wrote his German encyclical attacking Nazism root and branch and, when Hitler paid a visit to Mussolini, the Pope conspicuously went to Castel Gandolfo so as not to be in Rome at the same time as the Führer.

In 1939, appeasement failed. The war began. The Carmelites were very worried about the danger to Sister Teresa Benedicta. A nun she might be, but her blood was still Jewish. So in 1938 they moved her from Cologne to the Carmel at Echt in the Netherlands.

It was not far enough. Hitler's troops occupied Holland on 2 August 1942. The Gestapo invaded the Carmelite convent and arrested two nuns: Sister Teresa Benedicta and her sister Rosa. They were sent to the detention centre at Westerbork, where already over a thousand other Jews were imprisoned. Families had been broken up. No-one knew what would happen to them. The nun did what she could to comfort and console her people.

She could not see into the future, but she believed that when she reached the point where the horizon now stood, she would be able to meet whatever followed with peace. Thousands of men, women and children were crammed into railway trucks and despatched to the camp at Auschwitz.

On Sunday, 9 August, sixty years ago, Sister Teresa Benedicta walked into the gas chamber in which so many of her fellow-Jews and fellow-religious were to die. Had she lived she would very likely have been a great philosopher-saint of the Catholic faith; in her death she was certainly one of the martyrs of the Jewish faith.

Pope John Paul II canonised her, saying, 'Edith made her own the suffering of the Jewish people even as it reached its height in the barbarous Nazi persecution.' Along with St Catherine of Siena and St Bridget of Sweden he declared her a patroness of Europe, hoping it would raise in Europe 'a banner of respect, tolerance and acceptance which invites all men and women to understand and appreciate each other, transcending the ethnic, cultural and religious differences in order to form a truly fraternal society.'

It is her feast this coming Friday, 9th August, the anniversary of her death.

Chapter 16

I did not come to call the virtuous.

It was bad enough when Jesus recruited that quartet of Galilean fishermen: what on earth would they know of spiritual things!

Then he wanders along and sees – of all people –
a collaborator with the occupation forces: a tax-collector.
And recruits him – just like that. What criteria did he apply?
How did he interview those candidates for apostolic work?
How did he psychologically assess them?
How did he analyse the C.V.s?
In fact we don't know the full story.

My guess is that Jesus was by no means walking up
to total strangers. He would have done his homework.
He'd have observed the sons of Zebedee.
He'd have listened to what people were saying about
Jonah's boys, Simon and Andrew. He'd have sussed
out the true potential of Matthew, the tax collector.

You see, he wasn't judging achievement. He was
assessing potential. In some ways it's like university
selection – we are obsessed nowadays with grades
and apparently scientific methods of assessing
academic achievement, and we have come to believe
that examinations tell us all we need to know about
someone. That's bunkum.

Even if exams are totally accurate in measuring
achievement thus far, they are no true guide to the future.
For that you need a certain combination of insight,
and wisdom, and experience that looks beneath the surface
and assesses the possibilities of bringing out the best.

I find it instructive now, with the benefit of hindsight,
to look back on my own life. At ten I had a very high I.Q.
and sailed through the eleven-plus. But within two years
I had come unstuck. Why? Because boys need more
than intelligence to cope with schools.

At thirteen I was dumped into a backwater, destined
for early departure into office drudgery. And then,
by the grace of God, I found myself in the class
of an inspirational teacher. He was a young man
who didn't stay in teaching very long, but long enough
to look at me, unhappily floundering in his B-stream class,
and to decide I had potential. I can still clearly see
in my mind's eye the moment on Speech Day
in the corridor outside the Masters' Common Room
when he told my mother and myself that he saw no reason
why I shouldn't aim at Oxford.

I imagine that experience was pretty close to Matthew's.
Everyone accepted the conventional wisdom that his
destiny was scribbling away in ledgers at the customs'
house. Jesus came along – not with a magic eye, but
with shrewd judgment of character, and Jesus thought
that Matthew was capable of preaching and writing a Gospel.
What Jesus provided was shrewd perception of potential.

Later on in my life I had an experience of the opposite.
This time I wasn't the ugly duckling identified as a
future swan, but as a dead cert for promotion. It was
at the end of my first degree, and I apparently had all
the C.V. qualifications to be sent to Rome to study
for the priesthood: academic brightness, good knowledge
of Church history, pious and devout, and all the rest of it.
Put it all on the conveyor belt and end up
with a golden future as a bishop.

It never happened.

Within twelve months I had come unstuck and returned
to my spiritual anchorage in Oxford, and immersed myself
in academic life until I went rather quirkily to the BBC.
Only then, when I'd been for twenty years a tax collector,
did the Lord pass by again and say, 'Follow Me'.
And people said, 'You must be joking.'

What it proved to me is that vocation
is not to be judged as the world judges:
the Lord can and does reject the obvious candidates;
the Lord can and does transform unpromising material
into conduits of the Gospel.

Jesus went along to Matthew's house and met his friends
and ate with them – people who were deemed not quite
the thing by the very respectable. But people who could –
by the alchemy of love – be changed into pure gold.

It's true of aspiring evangelists – and it's true of all
of us. If we are so pleased with *ourselves* that we think
we are bound to be the chosen ones, we have left no
room for the grace of God. Only if we recognise that
the grace of God has much work to do in us can we
become pure gold.

If it's true on an individual level, it's also true of the
wider scene. In the 1960s and 1970s, many areas of society
were increasingly infected by a tragic delusion, and our
seminaries were affected as much as other institutions.
It was the delusion of 'doing your own thing', the
delusion of 'being your own self', the delusion that
'if that's how you are, that's how you ought to be'.

It's a sad delusion.
From that cataclysmic mistake have come so many
broken vows, so many sexual scandals, so much
self-centred infidelity, such a lot of deep unhappiness.

Our Lord did not come to canonise the self-satisfied, to approve the smug and self-deluding. He did not wish to keep us in our inadequacies, but to release our better selves with greater potential.

He did not want Matthew to do his own thing, but to do God's thing. He does not choose those who think they are ideally suited to the task already. He chooses those who will follow him in the hope that his mercy will transform them, and his grace will fill their hearts.

It is not enough to be ourselves; our hope is to discover our better selves through the mercy and grace of God.

Chapter 17

Some seeds fell on rich soil.

So – how am I supposed to turn myself into rich soil
that will enable the seeds of the Gospel to grow in my life?
To be honest, it's a bit odd thinking of ourselves as soil:
rather passive, rather inanimate. It doesn't seem a very
active vocation; soil just *is*. It reminds me of that song
about the new-fangled tango:

'You just sort of stand there, and just sort of *do* it.'

Easy enough for us to see ourselves as sheep or goats –
they do something! But soil – what does soil *do*?
Well, ask any gardener and you'll soon realise
how diverse soil is. Some soils are tricky because
they're too light and sandy or because they're dense
unforgiving clay, or too acid. *Gardeners' Question Time*
is forever telling us that what you need to do is to improve
the soil. They usually mean you've got to add something:
chemicals, compost, manure.

My granny believed that if you buried old razor blades
in the soil by the roots of hydrangeas you could alter
their colour. Well, be that as it may, the fact is that soil
can be enriched. And when we hear this parable of Jesus
it's not the seed we're bothering about, but the soil.
We are the soil and have to find ways of enriching it.
Soil has to take goodness in by absorbing the experience
of the seasons. All the seasons of our life help the soil:
the spring rains bring valuable minerals, the frost breaks
it up. The autumn leaves fall on it and melt and merge
into it. It just lies there, the soil ...

The way a lot of preachers talk you'd think that being
a Christian is always being active, full of crusading zeal,
hopping around to change the world. Plans of campaigns,
plans for 'renewal' conferences, and think-tanks, and
groups fizzing away like there's no tomorrow. But to
a large extent all that pursuit of action misses the point.
In fact there's not only *lots* of tomorrows but eternity
as well. The hectic pursuit of 'new initiatives' is a sort
of collective delusion which afflicts Christians every
now and again. It is often a sign of spiritual insecurity.

We shout at God and tell him what he's doing right
and how much better *we* could do it, and we fuss
so much about setting the Church to rights that we miss
the *point* of the Church – which is the Presence of God,
God among us. *Dieu parmi nous,* and we the absorbent
soil in which his word can grow.

We don't become rich soil by hyper-activity.
It's not what we *do* that matters but who we are.
The great contribution Basil Hume made to the
spiritual life of the nation was *who* he was.
Of course he did much good, but people perceived
that it flowed out of who he was: a man who
listened to God. He wasn't frenetic; he was serene.
He didn't know all the answers; he pondered prayerfully
to discover the questions.

When we remember him, we don't recall an agitator,
but a recollected man of prayer, gently putting the
real problems of the world into an eternal perspective.
So I suggest to you today that becoming rich soil is
achieved by prayer and contemplation and quiet
questioning. Instead of longing to be respected by
our fellow citizens for our contribution to charity

or our involvement in crusades, we would do better simply to want to become rich soil.

The delusion of our day, it seems to me, is wanting to 'express ourselves' and to be 'conspicuous in the sight of men'. We need to remember the Holy Father's wiser words: 'Man achieves the fullness of prayer, not when he expresses himself, but when he lets God be most fully present in prayer.'

As Jesus himself said: don't babble like the pagans do. We talk about *saying* our prayers. I prefer to talk about *listening* our prayers. Much prayer is show-off, boastful, self-congratulatory. Prayer needs to be self-effacing, and listening to the still small voice of God.

That's why the daily Mass is so helpful. For half an hour we can put ourselves gently into the presence of God, and listen to what he chooses to say. Listening is the first requirement of the spiritual life.

I went into the National Portrait Gallery a few days ago to look at the most recent portraits of the Great and the Good. Quite a zoo, really. Egos abounding. And in the middle of it all was the quiet figure of a snowy-haired man in a black cassock, sitting quietly apart, listening to God, listening to nature, listening to the *lacrymae rerum* – simply being in the presence of God. I try to keep that picture of Cardinal Hume in my mind. Let us persevere in prayer and remember when we pray that our words to God are important. But, more important still are the silences, when we listen and give God the chance to fill our hearts and minds with awareness of his presence.

To pray well is to listen carefully and that is how we enrich the soil we need to be.

*21 May 1988. On the forty-ninth anniversary of Fr Cormac's baptism,
Cardinal Basil Hume ordained him in Westminster Cathedral*

Chapter 18

The sound of a powerful wind from heaven.

So what does Pentecost mean?
It's a Greek word. It means the fiftieth day.

Originally it was a Jewish custom to mark
the fiftieth day after Passover by presenting
the first fruits of the corn harvest.
Then the Christians picked up the idea and ran with it,
because the day when the Holy Spirit electrified
the Apostles was the fiftieth day after Easter.

It took fifty days for the eleven disciples to recover
from the shock of seeing the crucified Lord rise from the dead
and to come to terms with that shock.

Fifty days to recognise that their world
could never be the same again.
Fifty days to realise that their restored faith in Jesus
could not be hugged to themselves but would
have to be proclaimed far and wide, wherever they could.
Fifty days to change themselves from a splinter group
in Israel to the world-embracing Catholic Church.

For me personally, the Vigil of Pentecost has a special resonance
because on that day I was ordained.
On Pentecost itself I said my first Masses.
I remember vividly when the white vestments of Eastertide
were graphically replaced by the red robes of Pentecost.
If you think that a big ceremony in Westminster Cathedral
is impressive when all the priests are in white,
you should just see it when they're all in red:
the building seems to glow so much
that it almost looks like it's on fire.

Any priest who has the good fortune to be ordained at Pentecost
is surely being challenged by the Holy Spirit
to be on fire with enthusiasm, to glow with warmth,
to 'melt the frozen, warm the chill'.

The Gospel Acclamation of Pentecost puts it in a nutshell:

'Come Holy Spirit, fill the hearts of the faithful
and kindle in them the fire of your love.'

When we hear St Luke struggling to convey the impact
of that fiftieth day, we hear a mix of sound and vision.
It sounded like a powerful wind – and my mind
immediately flies to the Atlantic coast.
I can see myself at Mizen Head at the extremity of Ireland,
the sun turning the ocean silver, and the wind slamming into me,
so that my chest is almost bursting with the freshness of it.
A sledgehammer wind that you can't see at all,
but which fills your lungs and roars around you
like a living thing – like the Holy Spirit, in fact.

And then the visual element.
Luke describes the apostles gathered together and a sort
of blaze appearing which broke into separate elements
and came to rest over the heads of each apostle like
tongues of fire – each one a candle in the wind,
once lit, never to be extinguished.

Watch a candle being lit. There it is, stolid and inanimate,
and then the fire approaches it and kindles it and the
candle begins to burn, using its energy to give light
and gradually, gradually, burning down.
And *there* is the image of vocation: a time of life,
an inanimate block of time, and *then* the fire touches it
and it begins to do what it was designed to do –
to give light and warmth and, in the process, to burn away.

There, by the altar, stands the current Paschal candle.
It came into use at the Easter Vigil.
But the old one still had some hours of burning left in it.
So I didn't throw it out. It has actually moved
a little closer to the Eucharist.
In the centre of the altar is a silvered-glass candle-holder
which I bought in Roundstone, County Galway,
and which I love to see in the centre of the altar.
Two years ago it was first used for a millennium candle.
Today it's being used for an old candle, a remnant,
something that might just have been thrown out.

I take encouragement from that.
When I was ordained fourteen years ago, my candle of life
was more than half burnt, but I have always taken heart
from lines by Gerard Manley Hopkins:

    'I have life before me still
    And thy purpose to fulfil
    Help me, Sir, and so I will.'

Left-over life to fill, plenty of warmth and life still to give.
There, in the Roundstone candle-holder,
is a retired Paschal candle still burning.

That's something we can all think about.
Spreading the faith isn't really arguments with unbelievers.
Spreading the faith is done by being the light of Christ
in the world; by giving light and giving warmth.
Each of us is a different candle.
Each of us has to bring warmth and light.
There is a variety of gifts but always the same Spirit.

On the feast of the Fiftieth Day we ask: what inspires us?
Each of us needs to be kindled by the Holy Spirit
so that as life's brief candle burns through,

the warmth and light it gives will gladden our hearts:

give us comfort when we die,
give us life with thee on high,
give us joys that never end.

'Come Holy Spirit, fill the hearts of your faithful
and kindle in them the fire of your love.'

Chapter 19

Look, there is the Lamb of God.

There is one person I know who is likely to end up
in Hell, and only one, and his name is Cormac Rigby.

When we think about Hell and all the wickedness
in the world, we imagine Hell to be overflowing –
but what a delusion that is. Who precisely is in Hell?
We don't know – and we can't know. Who precisely
is likely to go to Hell? Only one who deliberately
chooses to act against God's will.

I do not know anyone of whom I can say he, or she,
deliberately chose evil. I don't know – so I can't judge.
I may witness wrong acts but I have no means
of judging motives.

A man may steal from me – but it may be that his family
is starving. A man may curse me – but it may be
stress that fuels his anger. A man may hurt me –
but it may be those who long ago hurt him who
are the real cause of the hurt.

The simple truth is that I can judge no one's acts
but my own. I can resist an evil act but I cannot
presume to judge the man who did it; I do not
know how free was his choice. The only person
I know well enough to be able to say, he *chose* –
he deliberately *chose* – to do wrong is myself.
And so how do I judge myself?

We sometimes fall into the trap of presuming
that God is so merciful that he would never
let anyone go to Hell. We overlook the fact

that the choice is ours. We have the free will
to choose between good and evil. But I cannot
know how free any one else's choice has been.

I only know myself. And that is why I say
that Hell may be no vastness; that Hell may be
solitary confinement, for me.

Yes, I do believe in the mercy of God, but I also
believe that he has given me my freedom to choose.
I ask him to forgive the sins of my past and I hope
that in the future I may not make that fatal decision
to turn my back on God. But I also know that
because I am free and I am weak, I cannot presume
that I will not choose Hell. Each of us is the only
person who knows for certain whether or not we
have chosen good or evil.

Only I know my real motives. Only I perceive
the mix of goodness and selfishness in what I do.
And I know in the stillness of my own soul,
I know that I can sin, that I do sin, and that it is
always possible that, without the grace of God
to protect me, I can end up in a Hell of my own
choosing. What protects me from despair at
such a prospect is that I know the Lamb of God
has offered himself in sacrifice for me.

I know therefore that if I concentrate all my energies
on responding to God's grace and following Christ,
then I will at the Last Judgment be forgiven my
failures and be invited to be with God.
Each of us can say the same.

I know of only one person in grave danger of making
wrong choices. And I can plainly see that it is the
Lamb of God who died for me who stands between

me and the consequences of my wrong choices.
I cannot presume that God will forgive my wrong
choices. I am confident that he will give me the
grace to enable me to choose Him.

On 21 May 1988, Ted Rigby would have celebrated his 86th birthday. His wife Grace, widowed since 1969, received her son's first blessing.

Chapter 20

My prayer is that your love for each other
may increase more and more.

For the last couple of years I've done all the signing for
my Mother: forms, bills, cheques – all that sort of thing.
She has so little grip in her hands now that she can't
guide a pen properly.

But last week I was doing Christmas cards and I thought
it might be worth a try to see if she could just manage
a squiggle on cards to her old friends. So I put a big atlas
on her lap and found a biro that had more grip than most
and to my great delight she managed a very shaky but
very recognisable 'Grace'. And once she'd done one
there was no stopping her and before we knew where
we were she'd signed a dozen.

Each time, I identified the addressees and we had
a little natter to make sure she knew who it was for.
One was for a cousin of hers, a couple of years younger
and now in a nursing home in Devon, and when she signed
that one it wasn't 'Grace' she signed, but the nickname they'd
used as girls. So she was obviously thinking about what
she was doing and very clear about who was who. It was
all quite an effort, but each day last week we did a dozen.
For me, and I know for her too, each card was a prayer,
a prayer for the person it was going to.

What we were doing was thinking positively about individuals,
and that's what Christmas should be about – thinking a bit
more carefully about folk than we normally have time to do.
Thinking about them, remembering them, talking about
them, thinking about what we can do to show we love them.

Every aspect of Christmas can be a bit of a sham.
It's a battle to keep it from degenerating into an orgy of
greed and gluttony. Cards can be a drag, token gestures,
PR exercises, promoting a new line through robins and
mistletoe. But my Mother has always seen Christmas
cards as an assurance of her prayers, a reminder of her
love. It only takes a minute or two to sign a card, but
for the sender it's a little act of love and remembrance,
a chance to pray for someone, an opportunity to connect.
All through her life my mother has used the memory
cards in her prayerbook as a prompt for prayer and she
uses Christmas cards in the same way.

When Christmas cards get taken over by the advertising
men they lose their point. The firm pays the postage.
The secretary forges the boss's signature and the recipients
very sensibly bung them in the waste paper basket. But
we can use them as a promise of a prayer, as a token that
thought is being given. If we're really trying to put Christ
back into Christmas, then the Christmas card isn't an empty
gesture but a sign of remembrance and a promise of prayer.
We need to think of people and think prayerfully.

Let's be positive about our Christmas cards and remember
what St Paul wrote:

> Every time I pray for all of you, I pray with joy,
> remembering how you have helped to spread
> the Good News ...

> My prayer is that your love for one another
> may increase more and more and never stop
> improving your knowledge and deepening your perception,
> so that you can always recognise what is best.
> This will help you ... and prepare you for the Day of Christ.

Chapter 21

A light that darkness could not overpower.

The beginning of the year is a dangerous time
because it's so often an inducement to cynicism.
We make New Year's resolutions,
and before the year is a week old we've broken them.

The papers were full of hopes for 1994,
hope for peaceable integration in South Africa,
hope for an upswing in the economy,
hope for an end to violence in Ulster.
And then the death of another soldier
and another spate of firebombs dashes those hopes
and makes us feel really there's no hope.

And that's the danger – that we allow disappointment
over particular events to rob us of hope.
If we are to be realistic we must acknowledge
that disappointment is part of everyday experience.
It's bound to be so – we live with frail mortals
who are not expert in the art of love.

If our fallen nature inclines us to selfishness,
we are bound to cause disappointment to those who love us.
But disappointment is not the same as hopelessness.
As human beings we live in a climate of disappointment,
but as Christians we live in a climate of Hope.

We know that ultimately the Word of God
is more eloquent than any other word;
we know that the forgiveness of God
is more overwhelming than any lapse from grace.

We know that the love of God
is more durable than any other love.

We must distinguish between the virtue of Hope
and the emotion of optimism.
It's no bad thing to be an optimist –
I'm an incurable optimist myself –
but optimism isn't strong enough.
Optimism is just a feeling that things will go well.
Hope is more than that.

Optimism is a feeling that things will go well.
Hope is a conviction that even if things appear to be going badly,
good will nevertheless certainly come out of it.

Thirty years ago my hopes were dashed
as they had never been dashed before
and have never been dashed since.

I had been watching over a struggle for life
in intensive care of a friend of my youth,
badly hurt in a car crash.
And more than anything else I've ever wanted,
I wanted him to survive.

And on New Year's Day 1964, he lost the fight and died.
It took me a long time, years, to recover from
that disappointment, that apparent rejection of prayer.

It wasn't till much later, reflecting on all the good
that had come, both out of his life
and out of our struggle against death, that I began to understand
that optimism is a fragile thing, and that what we have to find
is not easy optimism but our abiding Hope.

Hope is the conviction that life has a purpose,
and that eternity is the ultimate reward,
the reward of life with God.

Hope is the conviction that God's purpose of love
is capable of fulfilment for all of us and that,
even out of heartbreak, he can create great good.
Hope is the deep understanding that God's light shines
not only in the sunlit heaven, but in the deepest dark;
and that it is a light that darkness cannot quench.

At his ordination Fr Cormac was presented by Joe Latham with one
of his splendid watercolours of Broadcasting House, where they had been colleagues.
Then Joe heard that Fr Cormac had actually been appointed to his own parish of
The Most Sacred Heart in Ruislip, and did this delightfully good-humoured
welcome card for his arrival there on 8.8.88.

Chapter 22

He makes the deaf hear and the dumb speak.

For a lot of people the idea of a 'life of prayer' is pretty sterile.

At the beginning of *A Midsummer Night's Dream,*
Hermia has fallen in love with Lysander –
who is not the husband chosen for her by her father.

Her father asks Duke Theseus to compel her to give up
her true love. And the Duke warns her that the laws of Athens
provide that young women who defy their fathers
may either be put to death or sent to a convent.

Death and the convent seem to be regarded with equal horror.
Bad to be put to death; just as bad to be confined to a nunnery.
That's how it seems to the outsider.

Some might see convent life as 'single blessedness'
but Theseus describes it as 'withering on the virgin thorn',
and he warns Hermia how awful it would be

> To live a barren sister all your life,
> Chanting faint hymns to the cold fruitless moon.

Help! Is *that* how *we* think of a life of prayer?
– barren, cold and fruitless?
Is prayer a running-away from this warm kind world?
Is prayer for monks and nuns but not for real people?

We can be deceived by popular images.
Every now and again a religious CD gets into the charts,
a CD of Gregorian chant maybe.
People who are bored by the Spice Girls turn instead
to the Incense Boys.

And religious pundits greet the news by babbling away
about how it all reveals a deep spiritual hunger.
How tranquil the music in the abbey sounds
to people caught up in the rat race!

And for a few well-marketed moments
the world changes its take on convents.
It used to hear nuns chanting and say how cold and fruitless.
Now it seems to hear monks chanting and say how cool!
But either way, the conclusion seems to be:
fine for them; irrelevant for me.

And yet we who are here at Mass today know
that the life of prayer isn't record-industry monks and nuns,
but our daily contact with our creator.

Prayer – in the old Catechism definition –
is the raising up of mind and heart to God.
And there are two sorts of prayer: speaking, and listening.
We need both. When we speak to God we articulate
our own deepest thoughts and aspirations.
When we listen to God we create silences
into which God can enter.

Prayer is both active and passive.
Active prayer is thoughtfulness.
It is thinking about our real purpose,
our human nature and our eventual destiny.
Thinking along such lines takes us into the world
of the spirit and opens our minds to perception of God.

Passive prayer is stillness.
It is allowing our hearts to open
to impulses deeper than our selfish hopes.
It permits our minds to reflect on the still small voice
which speaks into our silence.

And the best guide to both forms of prayer is Jesus.
He is, after all, the Word of God.
He is everything that God wishes to say to us.
And so our prayer must start and end with Jesus.

Whenever we pray – morning, noon or night;
wherever we pray – in church, home, or workplace,
it is best to begin with the Word of God –
a phrase will do, a single sentence, to trigger
a chain reaction of thoughtfulness in us.
And it is best to end with Jesus too.
'We ask this through Jesus Christ Our Lord, Amen.'

Prayer is our conversation with God.
Both he and I need to speak.
Both he and I need to listen.
I try not to interrupt him when he's talking
and he rarely interrupts when I'm talking.

So – what do I say?
I tell him first how great I think he is.

> You really are the one who made me,
> I am in awe of your power and goodness.
> I can see that you are the Shepherd and we are your sheep.
> I can see that we depend on you to choose for us
> the right paths and the most nourishing pastures.
> You are my true Father, the supreme being in eternity,
> and I salute you with all due reverence.
> I hope all your plans come to fruition.
> I know that what you want is always for the best,
> so what you want, I want.
> I want to consent to everything you do,
> both here and in the life to come.

That is my prayer of reverence, my praise of God.
What I've just said is in fact a paraphrase
of the first half of the *Our Father.*

It then goes on to the other aspect of my side of the
conversation – my requests, my longings, my hopes.

    I want to survive, to flourish, and grow, and deepen.
    I want to be fed each day.
    When I get things wrong I want to be forgiven,
    just as I hope I would forgive anyone who injured me.
    I'm pretty vulnerable, not very brave,
    and I want to be kept safe from all evil.

All this is me, putting into words the longings
of my heart, and it is a process of renewal because
even as I articulate my thoughts I am also refining them.

When I was a little boy I prayed for a complete collection
of Puffin books. When I was at school I wanted success.
When I was mature, I wanted wholeness and fulfilment.
And now that I'm nearly home, it's that homecoming
I pray for more than anything else.

Ask, says God, and you shall receive.
So I do ask, honestly and truthfully.
And when I have done asking, I remember
that now it's his turn; and in silence, or with Mozart,
or birdsong, I try to listen.
I've said all I can; now I need to listen to him.
Oh, that today I can listen to his voice; harden not my heart.

Jesus cured the dumb and the deaf –
that means us. You and me.
Dumb? I was tongue-tied, didn't know what to say.
Until I heard him say, 'Say what you mean,
say what you need to say, simply and honestly.'

And I am comprehensible to God, who is the perfect listener.

    For never anything can be amiss
    when simpleness and duty tender it.

That's the secret of prayer from our side – simpleness and duty.
Keep it simple; keep it regular.

We are no longer dumb, we are no longer deaf.
We speak in love; we hear the voice of love.
Love looks not with the eyes but with the mind.
And so, raising mind and heart to Love
cures us of our deafness and dumbness.
The life of prayer isn't fruitless chanting,
it is the daily conversation between God and us.

Chapter 23

How they had recognised him at the breaking of bread.

Every day of my life I enable a miracle to happen.
Some days twice, even more.
Today three times.

Not through any merit or ability of my own,
but because of a mandate given to me through
a succession of spiritual fathers and sons.

The mandate was originally spoken
two thousand years ago – and passed on to me
and to thousands of other priests.

Each day we are mandated by the Church
to take on the role of Christ and – in remembrance of him –
to take bread, and change it, as He did into Christ Himself.

At that moment at each Mass the miracle occurs,
which we call transubstantiation – the bread still looks
like bread but in its essence it becomes something other –
it becomes the body, blood, soul and divinity of Christ –
the Real Presence of Jesus of Nazareth,
true God and true Man.

It is a miracle – just as the Incarnation itself was a miracle.
Through this miracle, Jesus extends his presence on earth.
For thirty-three years the humanity of Jesus
was the focal point of the love of God in the world,
and since then, the real presence of Jesus
on the altar is the focal point of God's love
for every succeeding generation.

And the very shape the Church has evolved
for this bread describes the miracle perfectly.

It is a simple circle of white bread.
When it is elevated after the Consecration
so that we can all adore the Christ who is there,
it is as if we are looking up into eternity
with the help of a sacramental searchlight.

It probes into the unknown and holds for us
the vision of the eternal sacrifice of Jesus.
We look up, along that searching beam;
we see the perfect circle of white light, breaking
through the darkness into the eternity of truth.

And we see in our innermost eye, not a circle
of white bread, but the Light of the World,
focussing our attention on the eternal love of God.

As the Mass evolved from the meal –
the breaking of bread – into the Christ-centred worship
we know today, it became an enthroning
of Christ the King, it became an act of adoration,
of 'God-is-with-us'.
And the elevation is the moment when God in eternity
invites us to lift our eyes and see that sacrament divine
and bow our heads and say in adoration
'My Lord and my God'.

Years ago, there was a wonderful dancer
called Anna Pavlova.
She had genius, unique genius.
She danced with a grace and beauty that
transcended mere technique.

Many were the roles she danced, but the one
that was particularly hers was 'The Dying Swan'.
It was set to the poignant music of Saint-Saëns
and describes the death agony of that most graceful of birds.

Pavlova had the power to make you forget that
she was a ballerina – she *was* the dying swan.

On the night she died, the audience in the theatre
where she had so often performed was told the sad news
and then, while they were left with their memories,
the house lights were dimmed, the curtain went up,
and the orchestra played *Le Cygne*.

And the spotlight moved around the stage following
every move of the dancer who would dance no more,
allowing all those present somehow to see again
in that empty circle of light
the vision of that perfect beauty.

When I look at the white Host held up during Mass,
it reminds me of that spotlight, still following
the dancer who is no longer there.
And in that light the memory of a human life
continues to appear not just in the eyes of the beholder,
as in the theatre, but in the real presence beneath
that disguise of bread.

The Mass is the most sublime of the Church's treasures
because it puts the spotlight on the supreme sacrifice of Calvary.
It is the Dying Christ we see.
But there is this one wonderful difference.
In the theatre it was only a memory of Pavlova that was seen.
In the church it is the real and abiding presence
of Jesus of Nazareth.

'My Lord and My God.'

Chapter 24

But when the spirit of truth comes,
he will lead you to the complete truth.

These are words of Jesus that need to be thought through
very deeply, for they are the key to history.

What do I mean by that? I mean that the history
of the Church since Pentecost has been a learning process,
a process of discovery, deepening awareness,
an evolution of understanding, a mining operation
to discover the riches in the original deposit of truth.

It's profoundly important for Catholics to understand that.
People talk of being moved by the Spirit, of being inspired
by the Spirit in such a way that it sometimes sounds as
if a bright light is suddenly switched on for them and
they know it all.

But to know it all is something that is only possible
for God himself, and we should try to maintain a
much humbler notion of our understanding of God's truth.
The greatest enemies of truth are those who think they
have a monopoly of truth.

I remember being cornered in a tube train once by an earnest
evangelical who told me that, as a Catholic priest, I was a
perverter of God's truth. So I asked him, 'How do you
know what God's truth is?' And he said, 'I read the Bible'.
So I said, 'I read the Bible too'. But he said 'The Holy Spirit
fills me with the knowledge of all truth'. And I said,
'Well I'd never presume to think that the Holy Spirit
would reveal all truth to me. He leads my thoughts,

he inspires my meditation, and he guides my action,
but I'd never claim that he has revealed everything to *me*.'

Individuals may feel prompted by the Holy Spirit.
I frequently do, and I'm sure you do too.
But I'd never dare to elevate my own insights,
even my best insights, into a direct comparison
with the truth of God.

How can we know which of our ideas are genuinely
the inspiration of the Holy Spirit? There's only one way.
'*I* am the Way, the Truth and the Life', said Jesus of Nazareth.
And where is Jesus now? He sits at the right hand of God
and has sent the Spirit to be with his mystical body, the Church.
And in the Church we have access to the Truth.

So how can we suss it out? What is Truth?
I was told recently a very interesting fact about that question.
You remember, it was Pilate's question to Jesus:

> What is truth? *Quid est veritas?*

And if you shuffle the letters of those Latin words,
you can make another Latin sentence:

> *Quid est veritas?* What is truth?
> *Est vir qui adest.* It is the man who stands before you.

The answer to Pilate's question was actually there
in the question itself.

What is Truth? It is the man who stands before you.
Jesus is Truth and we come to the Truth when we know him.
So we need to listen to his words today:
'When the spirit of truth comes, he will lead you
to the complete truth'.

Jesus didn't say, 'The Spirit will have a word in your ear,
and then you'll understand the lot.'
He said, 'He will lead you to the complete truth.'

And through the Church we are indeed led towards truth
and the process is long, and deep, and part of history.
It took some years to sort out quite who Jesus was
and for the Holy Spirit to make it clear to the Church
that Jesus was true God and true man.
It took a few centuries to work out that Mary was not
just the mother of Jesus, but was therefore the mother of God.

You see what I'm getting at. The truth is there – a vast deposit
of many-faceted understanding, but it takes time and prayer
to investigate it and probe it and test it. And that isn't done
by one man in the tube train shone upon by the heavenly light.
It's done by the mystical body of Christ looking deep into its own
existence and experiencing the revelation of the Holy Spirit.

The teaching of the Church is the understanding of God
attained in its first two thousand years. There's a long way to go
before we can fathom the breadth and depth of God's truth,
but what has been revealed already is the tried and tested and
infallibly verified truth which Peter has set out for us.

In the magisterium, the teaching authority of the Church,
we see the Holy Spirit leading us towards the complete truth.
And on that magisterium we can prudently and safely
and confidently rely.

The Catechism of the Catholic Church is a treasury of the
spiritual discoveries made by the Church since Pentecost.
Incomplete, of course. The complete truth belongs in eternity
and no human words can express all that is in it. But make
no mistake. This *is* the essential work of the Holy Spirit.

This *is* the process of leading towards the complete truth
which Jesus promised. In the two-thousand-year history
of crystallising the truth, distilling the truth through thought
and prayer, this is a key moment.

What is truth? It is the man who stands before you. I am the truth. Feed my lambs, feed my sheep.

And we welcome this nourishing with all our hearts because in this nourishing we will grow.

Chapter 25

Today, my dear friends, on August 15th, we celebrate
the Resurrection. Let me say that again, to make sure
you heard what I'm saying: today is the great feast
of the Resurrection.

Earlier in the year we celebrated at Easter the rising
from the dead of our Lord and Saviour Jesus Christ.
And today, the feast of the Assumption, we celebrate
our own resurrection from the dead which will happen
for us in the future, as certainly as it has already
happened to Our Blessed Lady.

Our Lord was God and man and so it may be easier
for us to believe in his Resurrection. Anyone can
see that Almighty God is more powerful than death,
anyone can see that God is immortal. But Mary,
his mother, was a creature like us. Certainly she was
the purest of creatures, but a creature nonetheless.
The Queen of Heaven certainly, but a human like
ourselves. And for her the resurrection has happened
and is the pattern for our resurrection on the last day.

Mary has a unique place in our understanding of the mystery
of the Church. Her role in the unfolding story of the Church
springs out of her unique relationship with the Son of God.
As she was specially chosen by God to give human nature
to his Son, a perfect sinless human nature, she was
herself kept free from sin from the very beginning

of her human existence. The human nature she gave to
Jesus was unsullied by sin, untarnished by the inheritance
of all other children of Adam and Eve.

Her Immaculate Conception was the beginning of her perfect
life. And that perfect life of Mary is beautifully expressed
in one of the great documents of the Council, *Lumen Gentium*.

> Thus the Blessed Virgin advanced in her pilgrimage of faith
> and faithfully persevered in her union with her Son unto
> the Cross. There she stood in keeping with the divine plan,
> enduring the sufferings of Jesus with him, joining herself
> with his sacrifice and lovingly consenting to the immolation
> of this Victim, born of her.

And so she was given by her Son, as he was dying on the Cross,
as a mother to his disciple, with the words:
'Woman, behold your Son.'
At that moment Mary, who was the mother of God,
became the mother of all God's children.
Not just of John, the beloved disciple, but of all of us.

After her son's death, and resurrection and ascension,
Mary aided the beginnings of the Church by her prayers.
And finally, when the course of her earthly life was finished,
she was taken up, body and soul, into heavenly glory.
And, in the words of Pius XII, 'exalted by the Lord as Queen
over all things so that she might be the more conformed to
her Son, the Lord of Lords and conqueror of sin and death.'

In the Immaculate Conception Mary conquered sin,
in her Assumption into heaven Mary conquered death.
The Assumption of the Blessed Virgin is a singular
participation in the Resurrection of her Son and is the
anticipation of the resurrection of other Christians.

When we die, we have to endure that cleansing process which we call Purgatory before we can rise again. But Mary had no sins to be cleansed away and so no need for Purgatory, but rose at once to eternal heaven. Her Assumption is her resurrection, and the pattern for our resurrection.

We believe that the Holy Mother of God continues in heaven to exercise her maternal role on behalf of us all, the members of Christ's mystical body.

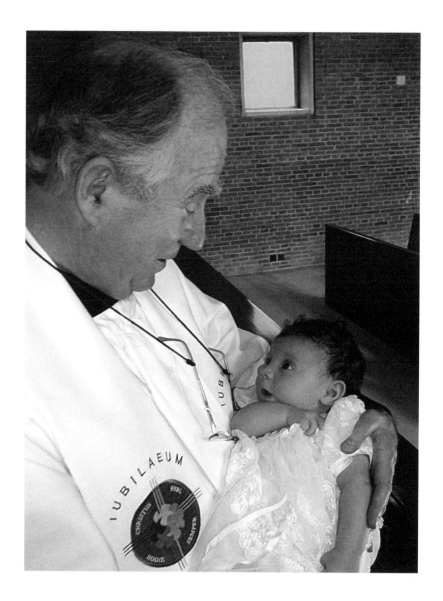

A baptism is the perfect opportunity to celebrate family.
Fr Cormac and Ellen-Marie Genower after her baptism
at St William of York.

Chapter 26

Baptise them in the name of the Father, and of the Son,
and of the Holy Spirit, and teach them to observe all I have
commanded you. I will be with you always, to the end of time.

Those are the final words of St Matthew's Gospel and they
form the most significant biblical text for the understanding
of the Trinity. When Jesus spoke those words, the apostles
who heard them had little idea what he was talking about.

We take that formula for granted: 'The Father, the Son
and the Holy Spirit.' We understand it as a way
of describing God. But it was an entirely new idea then –
it is, in fact, the great insight of Christianity.

Before the time of Christ, the Jewish people went
no further than the idea of the One God – the Lord.
It was not until Jesus came onto the scene, and until he
had revealed himself through his death and resurrection
as rather more than human, that the situation altered.
Jesus seemed to claim equality with the Father and he
also indicated that when he returned to the Father
(whatever that might mean) he would send a third party –
an advocate, a guide, an inspiration.

The baptism of John the Baptist was simply a baptism
of repentance. This baptism commanded by the Risen Lord
contains a much more profound idea
which is here formulated for the first time
and which would need centuries to be understood.
Not until nearly the end of the Second Century
did Theophilus of Antioch use the word 'Trinity'.

Not until the fourth-century Councils of Nicaea and
Constantinople was the doctrine defined in very simple terms.

The idea of the Trinity had to be developed gradually –
and the perceptions were slightly different in the East and the West.

In the West, the central idea was still that we believe
in *One* God. The one-ness of God is paramount.
But they had to sort out how this One God could involve
three separate persons: Father, Son and Holy Spirit.

St Augustine started from the way we human beings live.
He saw how we get to know ourselves and grow
to love ourselves and he tried to work God out from that.
The Son is the Father's knowing of himself and the
Spirit is the mutual love of Father and Son.
His thinking was taken up by St Thomas Aquinas
and definitively formulated.
It became the central doctrine of Christianity.

I remember when I was a boy hearing about St Patrick
preaching the faith in Ireland and trying to explain the Trinity:
Three in One. And Patrick picked up the little green plant
which had three leaflets in each leaf: the shamrock.
Three leaflets in one leaf. It's a reasonably good
way of explaining it.

But maybe there's another way which might help you.
It's rooted in the writings of the beloved disciple,
St John. His great slogan was 'God is Love'.
Now what do you understand from that? I suppose
it means that in some way God is the origin and inspiration
of all the love in the world, which is quite right.

But what does it actually mean? God is Love?
What do you mean by love? If I were to say to you:
'I love . . .' how would you understand that? I love. I *love*.
You look at me bemused and you say, well it all depends.
'I love . . .' doesn't actually mean anything.
It is an incomplete idea.

Until I tell you who or what I love,
you can't possibly know what I mean.
If I say, 'I love my Mother', that's very different from
'I love ice-cream'. You can only understand 'I love'
if you know who or what I love.

To understand love you need to know three Aspects of Love:
you need to know who is doing the loving, and what
sort of love it is, and who or what is being loved.
I love my friend: so from that you can deduce that we're
talking about a relationship, and love is a two-way traffic.
'I love ice-cream' is a one-way affair; I am not loved in
return. So to understand the meaning of love I have to
know three things: the lover, the loved one and the love
flowing between them. So, once you say 'God is Love'
you have to talk three, you have to talk Trinity.

When we inadequate human beings struggle to
understand what we mean when we say God is Love,
we are imagining God as a great eternal Energy of Love
which has always existed and which will always exist
and which comprises those three necessary Aspects of Love:
the lover, the loved one and the essence of love between them.

The Lover, the Loved One and the Spirit of Love; and we
normally call them the Father, the Son and the Holy Spirit.
As soon as we say 'God is Love', our language of Trinity
becomes necessary. That is the idea which helps unlock the
puzzle of the Trinity. If God is eternal Love, the three eternal
Aspects of Love are the Father, the Son and the Holy Spirit.
And it is in the name of that Holy Trinity that we baptise
and preach the good news.

There is no human way of describing God
which can possibly do justice to the Mystery.
But on this Trinity Sunday it is good to look at

the ancient formula at the climax of Matthew's Gospel and try to understand it a little more deeply.

The Father, the Creator, made us – but we lost our way and sinned. The Son, the Saviour, took flesh and died for us, redeemed us – but we still flounder; and so the Spirit, the Paraclete, the Comforter accompanies us on our journey to the end of time.

We are, each and every one of us, made in God's image, so we must learn to understand ourselves as the Creation and Continuity of Love.

God is Love; we are Love; I am Love.

It is my nature, and my eternal destiny.

Chapter 27

Many of his disciples left him
and stopped going with him.

How disheartening it must have been for Jesus to realise
that the gift he was offering to people – the gift of himself –
was beyond their comprehension.

They came when he worked a miracle to feed a crowd
because all they really wanted was a quick fix
for an immediate problem.
They had no interest in rising above that
to see to the distant horizon.

I can't blame them.
I'm too likely to be doing the same myself.
Too bothered about tomorrow to give thought to eternity.
Too likely to be a Martha when it's Mary I need to be.
I imagine it's the same with you and with most people.

Have you noticed how *Thought for the Day*
on the radio generally begins with some event in the news,
and then tries to find a link to God, or Jesus?

And that's the wrong way round.
It's starting out from some aspect of everyday life,
and then struggling to tease out a spiritual take on it.

By doing that we're trying to persuade ourselves
that we're speaking to the world, man to man.
Start with a car bomb, or a scandal, or a suicide
and try to find some religious gloss
that will make us seem aware and caring
about the concerns of our neighbour.

Increase the loaves and fishes
and Cafod becomes the religion.
I yield to no one in my admiration
for the work of Cafod – but what matters
is not its actual achievements but its motivation.

I remember the powerful words T S Eliot wrote
in *Murder in the Cathedral* about it being

> . . . the greatest treason:
> To do the right deed for the wrong reason.

Following Jesus for increased helpings
of bread and fish is a sort of treason.

It's motives that matter.
If we follow Jesus because he's Cafod man,
feeding the hungry, then our motivation
may be good but not as good as it ought to be.
It's Jesus, himself the bread of life, who really matters.

Peter – who so often got things wrong –
actually got this one absolutely right.
He realised that the people won over only by good works
wouldn't hang around once the appeal was over.

He could see that the people who set such store
on practical results would be bored with Jesus,
and would wander off again.

And when Jesus said to the Twelve
'Well – do you want to leave me too?'
it was dear old Peter who shook his head and said
'No – who else could we turn to?   You're the one
who has the message of eternal life and we believe.'

That is the true starting point.
God created life – and us.

He has a purpose for each of us
and he has a place for us with him in eternity.

If we start from God's love for us,
and work on loving God for his own sake,
that is the true priority. And then of course we'll find
all sorts of other loves springing from that.

Just think of the saints we're celebrating in the week ahead.
St Louis of France loved God so much
that he tried to be a truly Christian king,
bringing peace and justice to his subjects.

Blessed Dominic Barberi loved God so much
that he left his native Italy, and wandered the length
and breadth of foggy industrial Victorian England
in the hope of making converts.

St Monica loved God so much that she prayed
night and day for her prodigal son
to grow out of his wild youth and find God.

St Augustine loved God so much
that he devoted himself to theology,
and directed his mind to explore the mystery of Salvation.

St John the Baptist loved God so much
that he lived in the wilderness, and was not afraid
to challenge earthly power at the risk of his own life.

St Margaret Clitherow loved God so much
that she gave shelter to the priests who brought Christ
to his people – a housewife who became a martyr.

The starting point for all of them is their motive.
Our motive ought to reflect the first couple of questions
in the old *Penny Catechism*.

> *Who made you?* God made me.

Why did God make you? God made me to know him, love him and serve him in this world and to be happy with him forever in the next.

That's it. Our purpose. Our motive.
Not famine relief, not welfare; not any one of
a thousand things excellent in their own way,
but none of them as essential as knowing
who created me, and loving and serving him.

My thought for the day is not to make Jesus
relevant to the daily news, but to make my day
relevant to loving Jesus.

Many good things flow from loving God.
Loving God burns away our pride and deceitfulness.
Loving God opens our hearts to love of our siblings,
God's other children.

Loving God fulfils our purpose.
Loving God is the first priority of every day
because that is our reason for being.
'Love is my reason for loving'
– what a profound idea *that* is!

If my heart burns for love of God
it will give warmth to many others besides.
If my thoughts are full of God
that thoughtfulness will benefit many more.
If my anchorage is trust in God
then fear and anxiety can never disturb me.

Peter was later asked by Jesus:
'Simon, son of John – do you love me?'
'Yes, Lord.'
'Feed my lambs.'

He asked again: 'Do you love me?'
'Yes, you know I love you.'
'Look after my sheep.'

A third time Jesus pressed him – 'Do you love me?'
Poor old Peter was quite upset.
'Lord, you know everything, you *know* I love you.'
'Feed my sheep.'

The world tends to think that the first priority
for Christians ought to be feeding sheep.
But the real question is – 'Do you love me?'

And if we do, then the lambs and sheep need not worry.
If I truly love the Good Shepherd,
I will most certainly care for his sheep.

The Old School House, Uppingham

This is Fr Cormac's favourite picture. The drawing shows Edward Thring watching the flight of a swallow past the window of the Old School House at Uppingham. It was drawn by the art master, C Rossiter, to illustrate Thring's *Borth Lyrics*. An outbreak of typhoid in Uppingham had threatened to close the school down. Instead, Thring masterminded an exodus to Borth on the coast of Wales and the saga of Uppingham-by-the-Sea gave his work new life and a higher profile. Their going seemed like annihilation, but they were carrying seeds for the sowing; they came back, they came back full of song.

Twice Fr Cormac has been invited to preach from Thring's own pulpit in the Chapel at Uppingham: on 12 June 1977 for the Borth centenary, and 22 October 1987 for the centenary of Thring's death. His research for his doctorate had included reading the manuscripts of all the sermons Thring had preached to his boys from 1853 to 1887. And so when he was himself ordained in 1988, it made sense to reprint this evocative drawing at the end of the Order of Service. Fr Cormac had worked behind those windows, absorbing the power of Thring's words and finding them still potent a century later.

Sweep, glorious wings, adown the wind;
    fly, swallow, to the West,
Before thee, life and liberty;
    behind, a ruined nest.
Blow, freshening breeze, sweep, rapid wing,
    for all the winds are thine,
      The nest is only clay.
The rapid wings were stretched in flight,
    the swallow sped away,
And left its nest beneath the eaves,
    the much-loved bit of clay,
Turned with the sun, to go
    where'er the happy sun might shine,
      And passed into the day.

Borth Lyrics, Prologue

Edward Thring, born Somerset 1821. Captain of the School at Eton, Fellow of King's College, Cambridge, Headmaster of Uppingham 1853–1887. His writings (*Education and School*, 1864 and *Theory and Practice of Teaching*, 1883) were influential. But it was the living example of Uppingham that enabled him to become the teachers' teacher. He is the real hero of the 1912 school-novel *Fathers of Men*. Its author was E W Hornung, writer of the Raffles stories, who had been a boy at Uppingham. "For 'Jerry Thrale' ", wrote Hornung, "read 'Teddy Thring' – and behold that great man as he appeared to one of the rank and file of the school towards the close of his devoted career." Thring's whole life centred on his faith:

> *Christ present, Christ living,*
> *Christ with us in our life day by day*
> *Turns that life at once*
> *Into a thrilling, a sacred gift, and*
> *Will make the spirit of the past living too*
> *And pour it into our lives*
> *With living power.*

Chapter 28

*Edward Thring Centenary Sermon, preached in
Uppingham School Chapel, 22 October 1987.*

Here, in this Chapel, here above all we mustn't get it wrong. If you are looking for a monument to an architect, look around. But if it's Edward Thring you're looking for, he is not here. He spoke of the 'almighty wall', but he is not within these walls. He's not even in that wonderful statue outside, which captures so strikingly the alertness and the tenseness and the authority of the man. He is not to be found in memorials, and this is not a panegyric.

I can sense those brilliant blue eyes staring at me, and I can hear him snapping out those words he wrote in his diary in 1859: 'Let no one write Latin humbug or English either over my bones. No word of praise or blame if they love me.'

There is nothing now visible of Edward Thring. When one of his contemporaries died, a mutual friend said to him that the man's work would now come to nothing. 'Well', said Thring, 'his work is in the hearts he has won. The visible work probably won't go on. *This* is not going to go on.'

He caused this Chapel to be built because he wanted a symbol of the beliefs that stood at the heart of his life's work. He would not thank us for identifying him with bricks and mortar, or by speaking of his life as a success because he ended it as a celebrity.

His work was in the hearts he had won. His work was teaching, and his great educational experiment was to prove that teaching was an act of love, an act of thinking love. Do we still honour that belief? Does he still speak to us a century after his death? If he is here, he is present not in the buildings but in the life that is lived here.

His own schooldays, at Ilminster and Eton, had been a shocking contrast with the happy and encouraging home life he had enjoyed in Somerset. He saw the majority of young lives made miserable by a cruel and wasteful system. He determined to show in his life as a teacher that the first task is to discover the potential there is in every single child, and the second task is to find ways and means to develop it: good machinery, as he would put it.

So here at Uppingham he assembled a band of fellow workers who created a small kingdom of good buildings and a good environment, to support a varied curriculum and a strong sense of educational purpose. The consequent financial burden crippled him for the rest of his life. He could so easily have run the school at a profit if he had only sacrificed his ideals and allowed the weak to go to the wall. But he would not; he would have died first.

When typhoid broke out in the town, he was faced with ruin. But he met the crisis bravely and created Uppingham-by-the-Sea at Borth, in a year of improvised enterprise that captured the imagination of the whole profession. It gave him the moral authority to fight bitter battles with politicians, governors and trustees who challenged his educational priorities. He joined forces with other headmasters; he helped unite the teachers against the government policy of thinking that education could be validly measured by examination results. And he wrote a textbook on teaching which puzzled and inspired a whole generation of teachers.

It frequently meant conflict. He was on occasions wilful, autocratic, unfair. He was sometimes wrong. But he was never, never ungenerous. When he attacked, it was the powerful and the privileged he had in his sights. He was the defender of the young, the exploited, the vulnerable, and all those whose lives were bought and sold to satisfy the greed of the well-endowed.

What spurred him on was his love of life. *Life* was his mantra. He saw this school as 'a mighty centre of possible life'. 'Life', he said, 'divine life, must be up and doing in God's great world or it is not life. As far as it shrinks, and shuts itself up, and draws back, and fears, and seeks shelter, it is not life, any more than running away from an enemy is courage.'

His Christian faith was rooted in the theology of the Incarnation. The Hebrew Testament had shown how man had learnt to worship

God through laws and liturgy, but then God became man in order to demonstrate to humanity that true worship is the living of a life:

> Divine life became incarnate in man, incarnate in you; and living out truth, that is Christianity. Nothing else is. No Gospel book is Christianity, no teaching is Christianity, nay more, no sacraments are Christianity. We must have them all, but ... there is no true Christianity where the new life does not pass out into doing good to others and with others as its main life.

The Chapel symbolised for him the fact that all the little decisions in life are a choice for good or evil. If every decision were to be made in favour of the good and the creative and the selfless, the cumulative effect would be to transform life. He didn't urge heroic gestures on big occasions; he preached daily fidelity and constant effort. No one was too insignificant to feel part of the great unbroken life, to feel that each of us belongs to it, 'that the little boy in the 1st or 2nd form is important, that the dull unsuccessful worker is important, that the idleness of the idle is fearfully important, that the quiet manliness of the humblest of us here is important. We want to feel not that the sea is large, but that every drop in the sea is a life and a power. No drop is more important than another. Those that seem least so, those that vanish into air, become rain, and rivers, and fountains, the life of life to the world.'

Now we begin to see what Thring was getting at. Any fool can pour knowledge into a clever boy. Any fool can express noble sentiments about mankind. But to teach effectively, to live creatively, you have to love an individual. And that means that you first have to get to know the individual and discover what it is that will enable that individual to flourish. First understand, then act.

Another great teacher, Pestalozzi, used to say that the essential principle of education was not teaching, but love. Thring added a crucial word: 'a thinking love'.

Uppingham was intended to be a place where thinking love operated: where there was a Chapel to inspire and unite; a gymnasium to strengthen;

a sanatorium to heal; playing fields, a pool, gardens, an aviary, laboratories, classrooms, workshops, private studies, music rooms, tishes. So that honour could be given to lessons and every pupil would have the chance to make something of the life God had given.

> Noble character is trained by noble example of life, whether in word or deed, and by honest surroundings, whether in word or deed. The highest beliefs and the most true work train noble character . . . the hearts of the teachers are all in all.

Edward Thring believed that God's will is only another name for man's happiness. I have read all the sermons he preached in this Chapel from 1853 to 1887, and the paragraph that strikes me as most quintessentially Thring is this:

> There is nothing more characteristic of God on earth than the boundless liberality with which he has scattered little pleasures in everybody's reach. But if this is so, then man most imitates God when he gives in this Almighty way, when he opens and makes free, and scatters pleasure as God does, and makes it possible for others to be glad.

On the evening of Saturday, 15th October 1887, Thring sat at his desk as usual to pour onto paper the sermon he was going to preach next evening. But on the Sunday morning he was unwell and had to leave the Chapel during the service. His condition worsened; for a few days he struggled for life, but soon after dawn on 22nd October the end came, calmly and peacefully.

On his desk they found his diary. The last entry written late on the night before he was taken ill was a fairly typical mix of irritations and blessings. But the day had ended on a note of optimism:

> and now to bed, Sermon finished,
> and a blessed feeling of Sunday coming

The sermon itself lay between sheets of blotting paper on the desk. The final words, which Edward Thring did not live to utter, I will speak to you now, a century later:

Nay brethren, in Christ all things
have become holy that he gives.

Take, then, his gifts and use them worthily
in his kingdom of love.

The church of St William of York at Stanmore, designed by Hector Corfiato and dedicated by Cardinal William Godfrey. The feast of St William is on 8 June.

Chapter 29

He instructed them to take nothing
for the journey – except a staff.

That's one of those phrases that always gets to me.
I am notoriously incapable of travelling light.

I'm just not the sort of person who can cram
all his worldly goods into an overnight bag.
And of course when I set off for Ireland, the boot is
also weighed down with the books I intend to read.

So, taking nothing for the journey is not my style.
I console myself with the thought that what Jesus is really
talking about here is not so much the spare shirt and the books,
but our attitude to possessions and to the unexpected.

Possessions can be a great snare. We become so fond of
what we own that ownership defines us. And if we value
possessions for their own sake, that is a kind of idolatry.
Possessions are only worth having if we take a genuine
delight in sharing them.

If we want to live a Gospel life of love, we do have
to eradicate possessiveness and enjoy sharing all we have.
That's certainly part of what Jesus was getting at.

But there's a second aspect to what he was saying.
Travel through life in such a way that you are not thrown
off course by the unexpected. Travel light in that sense.

We all have our own plans – but we also know that God has his,
and it is important to trust in his providence.
I would never argue that some evil happening must somehow
be the will of God: that would be a terrible blasphemy.

But what is certain is that every bad situation can be turned
to good purposes through the grace of God.
And that helps us to adapt to circumstances.

When I first tried to be a priest, in 1961, it all came rapidly unstuck.
I left the seminary within a year and it felt like a disaster, a setback,
a blow, a disappointment, the end of all my hopes. But with the
benefit of hindsight I can see now what God saw then:
that I needed a much longer and rather different formation
from the one I had envisaged.

I feel much the same about the situation I find myself in now.

At the beginning of last year a routine medical check-up
showed indications of prostate cancer – but, as I told you then,
there were no symptoms, and two biopsies failed to discover it.
However, you will remember I had a couple of episodes last
November when I ended up in Accident & Emergency
with back pain.

At the beginning of this year, after a couple of MRI scans,
the diagnosis was made that there was indeed cancer in the prostate
and that it had now spread to my back, the pelvis and the spine.
I have been having monthly injections since January which are
helping to keep it at bay.

Of course, it will be my strategy to live as fully as possible for
as long as possible. But I had to think about the implications
for the parish. What happens if I have a sudden bad day?
Imagine the disruption to a wedding or a funeral. And with
a major building programme expected next year you need
the priest to be on hand.

It is not what I had foreseen or hoped for, but one has
to be flexible and to respond to events as they happen.
The usual time for priests to be moved is in the summer,
so if serious thought was to be given to it, the bishop

needs to know as soon as possible. So on Ash Wednesday
I went up to Westminster to see Bishop George Stack, the
auxiliary responsible for our deanery, and put him in the
picture – and he has been wonderfully supportive to me.
He has been able to find the man we need in Stanmore
and I am very happy, and relieved, that this has happened.

Canon Michael Roberts, who is at present Parish Priest
at Buntingford, will be taking over from me in September.
He is a lovely man – exactly the same age as myself –
a calm and gentle and good-humoured man, and a holy
and learned priest. He actually taught me while I was
at the seminary and while he was at St Edmund's, Ware.
So I am greatly consoled by the knowledge that you
will be getting a most excellent priest to lead you on.

Regrets? Yes, of course. I have loved every minute of my
time here. But I remember the difficulties when I first came:
my predecessor had died in office, there was a long gap and
I had no handover. This time, by the grace of God, we've
been able to avoid such a hiatus and I can hand over to
Michael in a tidy way and retire to meet my own destiny.

I ask you to see it as I see it. All through life we live in
awareness of death and, as our faith deepens, so does our
confidence that death is simply the doorway to God's kingdom.

At each Requiem I have said this year I have found myself
asking, in the light of my own circumstances, do I actually
believe in my heart what I profess in my words.
And I have discovered that I do.

Faith does not remove difficulties; but it enables us to
cope with them. I would like the next two months to be
as normal as possible and I am sure you will help me.
In the time before I leave in September I will need your prayers.
And when I have left, I'll need them even more.

On this occasion, in these circumstances, I know I have to travel light. I know I will be taking nothing for this journey except my staff.

But that staff is the Faith and the power of prayer, and I can lean on that staff until I have safely reached journey's end.